Cousin Camp Manual

Wisdom Workouts To Strengthen

Family Ties

Peggy Miracle Consolver, Author

Caitlin Rose Consolver, Contributor

Carpenter's Son Publishing

Cousin Camp Manual: Wisdom Workouts to Strengthen Family Ties

© 2022 Peggy Miracle Consolver

Published by Carpenter's Son Publishing, Franklin, Tennessee

Published in association with Larry Carpenter of Christian Book Services, LLC
www.christianbookservices.com

Cover and interior design by Suzanne Lawing

Printed in the United States of America

978-1-952025-84-6

Preface

This Cousin Camp Manual has been a labor of love. It is the culmination of sixteen years of annual cousin camps for our five grandchildren. I am thankful for the prior experiences of being a counsellor at Girl Scout camps, for being a Girl Scout leader seven years, helping at Cub Scout and Girl Scout day camps, teaching and organizing our church's Vacation Bible Schools, and thirty-seven years of teaching Sunday school.

I have always delighted in teaching children—ever since the first VBS when one little boy heard about Shadrach, Meshach, and a-billy-goat.

Children are such delightful creatures! I could not miss the opportunity to get to know my own grandchildren and make a contribution to their lives.

Six reasons I put together cousin camps for my children and grandchildren:

1. So I could get to know my grandchildren on a deeper level as they grew.

2. So they would know each other.

3. So I could provide our children and their spouses this gift of a small amount of time each summer to have just for each other.

4. So I could share my faith with my grandchildren.

5. So I could share our heritage with our grandchildren.

6. So our grandchildren would know they would never be alone in navigating this sometimes crazy world.

The rewards far outweigh the costs.

Sincerely,

Peggy Consolver, Author
PeggyConsolver.com
Shepherd, Potter, Spy—and the Star Namer, novel 2015
The Star Namer and the Unchosen, novel 2019
Star Namer Bible Study: Joshua 9 & 10, 2021
Kacey's Question, picture book 2018

NOTE TO THE USER: Whether you are working from a hardcopy edition OR from a digital version, if any of these links are inactive, please go to PeggyConsolver.com and click on "Cousin Camp Manual/Bibliography. These internet links will be tested periodically by the author and suitable substitute links provided. ENJOY THE ADVENTURE OF COUSIN CAMP!

Acknowledgements

Each "cousin camp" we did through the years, sixteen of them, was the stuff that memories are made of. As I brought out old files from the early days, I remembered the special times we spent together at our humble lakehouse. God blessed those days. *Thank you, Lord.*

We were in the year 2020, when for the first time Cousin Camp did not happen, that this *Cousin Camp Manual* began to take shape. Because of Covid-19, our oldest grandchild was available to do a sort of internship for this *CCM*. She is the same one who got me started writing in 2006 when she was seven years old. I had observed her since she was two as she pored over picture books to get the meaning when she could not read a word.

At seven she had just read her first chapter book. She was so excited she bounced as she told me she wanted to be an author when she grew up. She wanted to write stories!

Her words reverberated in me.

So, thank you, Caitlin, for getting me started writing fifteen years ago.

And now she had only one more year to complete a degree in writing. Thank you, Caitlin, for researching and writing the Foreword and assisting me in the summer of 2020 as you interviewed every participant in our sixteen years of Cousin Camps. You captured on paper their most closely held memories. I believe the quotes from your interviews that are included in the "shadow boxes" within this work serve to illuminate further the importance of the Cousin Camp experience in the lives of all our family.

Thank you, Caitlin, for your valuable contribution to *Cousin Camp Manual: Wisdom Workouts to Strengthen Family Ties.*

Foreword

By Caitlin Rose Consolver

Most Americans don't know their cousins.

Ask around, and it's rare to find a person over the age of twenty-five who sees their cousins more than once every few years, if at all.

Why?

Because Americans are busy, and busy people will not make time for what they do not value. America, in general, doesn't prize distant family connections the way it used to.

And that's a problem. In the article "The Nuclear Family Was a Mistake" by David Brooks, one might be expecting to find a piece arguing against the validity of the traditional family structure. But it's the isolation of the traditional nuclear family of two parents with children from the support of extended family that is the concern. Brooks is **arguing** *for strengthening extended family connections.*

For millennia, extended families living in close proximity were extremely important, an integral function of society. Nursing homes were not a thing; multi-generational housing was the norm. Moving typically meant saying good-bye to everything and everyone you had ever known and stepping into a completely foreign way of life. So, it was a rare thing indeed to move. In all likelihood, all your cousins would live only a few miles away. But in the past century, a lot has changed that has not only weakened the extended family, but the close-in family unit at the same time.

Today, there is a distinct lack of close relationships between members of the extended family. Moving far from family and friends has become commonplace, and multi-generational housing is a thing of the past. While "connecting" through technology has become easy, it cannot replace time spent face-to-face. There's a reason why long-distance relationships are hard. A reason why you didn't keep in touch like you planned with the friend who moved away. Technology simply cannot provide the same experience as being with someone in-person.

My family has had the good fortune to live relatively close. We have no family members that live across an ocean. The cousins detailed in this book live only an hour away, or less when the traffic isn't bad. But even an hour can seem awfully far away when dealing with a hectic schedule.

Cousin Camp provided us an opportunity to step back from the real world once a year and spend a few days focusing on our relationships with each other. It allowed us to build real connections rather than superficial ones. It was of the utmost importance in granting us the opportunity to truly know one another and be family, not just blood relatives, but *family*.

In doing research for this manual, I came across another article whose title intrigued me, "7 Reasons Why Cousins Are The Most Important Part Of The Family Unit" by D. Joyner on BlavityNews.com. Cousins, the most important part of the family unit? More so than siblings, parents or grandparents?

The article contained seven main points, but three in particular caught my eye. The first point is that the larger family can become of key importance when a family member is lost. The extended family of well-bonded cousins can gather round and support each other in times of grief and can be a stronghold. The second is that cousins are often lifelong friends, and more likely to be so than other friends. Family is family forever; once formed, you can't lose that connection. Therefore, it is much easier to establish and maintain a relationship with a cousin that you have known since childhood. No matter how much time or distance parts you, the familial connection remains and can serve to keep you anchored together. Family is about more than just blood; it's about love, trust and growth. A bond forged between cousins early on is vital, because without establishing that connection early in life, cousins who don't know each other may not consider each other family at all.

But the point that really stuck with me was the third: that the role of cousins can be similar to the role of siblings, particularly if one of the cousins is an only child. While I myself am not an only child, I have no sister. However, I always wanted one, particularly in my early years, before my brother and I became close. My cousin Presley was able to be that for me.

Despite our six-and-a-half-year age difference (the half can be so important when you're little), we have always connected easily. While we may not see as much of each other as sisters do, I think our time together was reflective of the best moments a pair of sisters might share, without all the drama-filled moments in between. Cousin Camp was vital in cementing that relationship. Presley herself said, "I think it's really beneficial to make sure that we all create relationships. We definitely needed Cousin Camp for that."

Family is important, so *knowing* your family is important. Mothers and fathers and siblings and grandparents are important, and so are aunts and uncles and cousins. Family is family, extended or not, and family is the framework of love and support in our lives. The foundation of who we are and who we strive to be.

What Cousin Camp accomplishes can be summarized in a single sentence: It allows children to know their family. And not just family members, but also the ties that bind the family together. The foundation of the family: what your family believes in.

Throughout childhood, we are instilled with family values. How to treat others, how to get along with people we don't like, what we should and should not do, what is good for us and what is not. Cousin Camp was like boot camp for family values. Not all cousins got along well; we had to go out of our comfort zones and learn to share and compromise. We were in very tight quarters, and privacy was considerably lacking (but thank goodness, we had more than one bathroom).

God was a hugely important cornerstone of Cousin Camp every year, as the identity of our family is centered around Christ.

Grammy always told us that one of her major goals in life was to know that all her grandchildren would be with her in heaven. We had all accepted Christ by the age of ten. Cousin Camp was far from the only place where we were exposed to Christian teachings. Cousin Camp could be likened to VBS (Vacation Bible School) in its ability to expand our knowledge of God and understand His love for us so much better in a single week. We had Bible studies every morning and talked about Christian and Biblical concepts. And every year, at the end of the week we would have a big show for the parents, usually with magic, short skits, presentations of our art projects, and scenes from the Bible. One year we even acted out the story of Esther, my own personal favorite book of the Bible, though in retrospect Grammy had to censor the storyline a little for us to make it age appropriate.

A great deal of Cousin Camp was reserved for education. Every year, there was some kind of theme to focus on; one year the theme was space, and we learned about everything from the way astronauts lived to building our own rockets. These educational pursuits turned Cousin Camp into (fun) crash courses that put us ahead of the pack in school, while simultaneously serving as a bonding activity.

"For several years as Grammy read through her Bible chronologically, when she came to the N.T. she would switch to a new Bible to give to a grandchild at Christmas. She prayed for that grandchild and underlined important verses throughout the Bible as she read." (GC)

Throughout the years, we did simple things, exploring the lake shore, or finding a little island we claimed like pioneers. We would look for fossils and little samples of ancient marine life which were abundant. And then, we took looking for ancient objects to the extreme when we flew halfway across the world to volunteer for an archaeological dig in Shiloh, Israel. The family spent a week digging all day long in the dirt under the hot summer sun. It was grueling, it was exhausting, it was tedious, and it was *incredible*. There is nothing more fascinating than ancient times. Nothing to be more proud of than the search for the truth. And cousins doing it together made it all the more special.

Cousin Camp was an amazing part of my childhood, and one that holds many of my fondest and clearest memories of my early years. It was a place to learn, to grow, to explore, and most importantly, to connect. In our society, cousin relationships are not considered as important as they once were. That needs to change. Cousins can be an incredible blessing. Holding a special time every year for cousins to get together will foster some of the most treasured memories and relationships in the lives of everyone involved.

Contents

Keys to
A Meaningful Experience

Key Goal

Strengthen Family Ties with Rich Experiences Together

Do you have memories of childhood times spent with cousins, and you still smile when they come to mind? Perhaps "in the olden days" when scads of cousins lived and worshiped in a relatively small area—at least in the same state, those times occurred naturally. Perhaps a few times a year you got together with cousins when grandparents and even great-grandparents celebrated an anniversary or holiday. In this day of widely separated family units, together times need to be more intentional.

> "If we didn't have Cousin Camp, we wouldn't be this close." PK/14

We've seen it in your eyes at our mention of "cousin camp." That spark of deep desire to be connected with your grandchildren or siblings and nieces and nephews and to give that gift to your own family. Beyond your children's developing tangible long-lasting relationships with cousins, they will begin developing an intangible gratefulness for their common heritage and a grounded-ness they need as this fluid society swirls around them. In a time of the rapid breakdown of the nuclear family, we are praying God will use your efforts and ours to strengthen the ties of mutual support among family members through this extended family project.

A worthy immediate goal for cousin camp is that each child, each year, will return home a little more mature—a little less dependent and clingy than before. When they experience a few days without mom or dad in a safe and secure loving atmosphere, they become

> A top memory of all the boys: "piling onto each other ... making a stack of three sitting on each other's shoulders in the water." CR

"At the end-of-Cousin-Camp celebration party we had a special meal that the kids had helped with." CA

a little more confident in their own abilities and a little more experienced at helping and cooperating with others.

Of course, some of these goals can be partially achieved in similar situations like scout camps, day camps and retreats or church youth camps. But we're talking about family here.

There are plenty of opportunities to grow independence independently, but to grow f-a-m-i-l-y is a totally other thing.

Investing your prayers and time and resources in building up your family is perhaps one of the very best investments you can make. We'd like to give you a starting point that is highly adaptable to your own unique situation, number of participants, and adult helpers available.

Come along for an adventure that will fuel a lifetime of warm family memories for your children and/or grandchildren.

Key Goals at Cousin Camp

- **To strengthen the bond of the cousins** with shared memories.

- **To strengthen our families** by working together on this Cousin Camp Project.

- **To give the cousins rich experiences** that will enhance their self-esteem, success in the classroom, and indeed, in life.

- **To offer the cousins a wide variety of experiences** in different settings and activities with the mutual support of family—thereby taking away, or at least lessening, the fear of trying new things. For example: exploring the outdoors hiking, fishing, camping, at a zoo, or sports event. Or introducing a new skill or hobby such as golf, archery, art, sewing, music, or others!

"Cousin Camp was very intentional to bring family together; otherwise, it just doesn't happen." BW

- **To grow healthy well-adjusted individuals.**

- **To the degree you are free to do so, share the gospel and your faith by word and deed in every aspect of Cousin Camp.**

In a very real way, a cousin camp with these goals can be the working out of our faith and delivering in a nutshell an opportunity for our kids to experience our Theme Verse.

"Truly priceless: the importance of stories/memories of the 'epic battles' of cousin camp." AA

"And Jesus grew in wisdom and stature
And in favor with God and men."

Luke 2:52

Key to Success
The Support of All the Parents

Cousin camp cannot be a "little red hen" operation. Winning the support of other family members will be your first step to get started. Adequate adult supervision on site during all activities is essential. You cannot go forward without it. Of course, most everyone will welcome a few days of break from—*ahem*—for the kids. But the point is, you will need one or more adults with you. Who will that be?

> "I appreciate Grammy's big vision for our family." DK

A sidekick for the whole camp, a different assistant each day, or whatever you come up with. Use the layout below to help others catch the vision for this cooperative effort project.

The meaning behind the title of "Wisdom Workouts" comes from Luke 2:52 describing Jesus' life as a young boy.

Luke 2:52, "And Jesus grew in wisdom and stature, and in favor with God and men."

Wisdom	Stature	Favor
Learn about God and His Son Jesus.	Eat good food.	Respect others.
Learn about God's creation.	Get outdoors.	Use good manners.
Learn about history and family.	Get plenty of rest.	Be helpful.
Make good decisions that please God.	Practice safety rules.	Cooperate.

Wisdom Verse:

"The fear of the Lord is the beginning of wisdom, and knowledge of the Holy One is understanding."

<small>PROVERBS 9:10</small>

Stature Verse:

"For You created my inmost being; you knit me together in my mother's womb. I praise You because I am fearfully and wonderfully made."

<small>PSALM 139:13-14</small>

Favor Verses:

FAVOR WITH GOD: *"Let love and faithfulness never leave you . . . Then you will win favor and a good name in the sight of God and man."*

<small>PROVERBS 3:3-4</small>

FAVOR WITH MAN: *"[Wisdom is] "doing what is right and just and fair."*

<small>PROVERBS 1:3B</small>

Key to a Smooth Operation

Planning, Preparation & Communication

Number 1 is: The Leadership Team gets started—EARLY!

Nov/Dec	Jan	Feb/Mar	April	May	June/ July
(Talk About it)	Dir & Co Committed.	Query All/ Plan/Set Date	Letter/ Parents	Letter/ Cousins	Cousin Camp!

When? Where? How Much? How Long?

Starting early, set your own summer calendar non-negotiables, reserving important dates for your own family/household. Enlist a sibling or cousin or aunt to be co-coordinator who will do the same.

Together, you will research the possibilities, choose a site you are comfortable with, develop a theme or use the "Wisdom Workouts" suggested here, do the preparation legwork, take the heat literally and figuratively! You will be on site for the whole camp, be intimately involved with the kids, experience the pitfalls, reap the blessings, and learn from it.

Where do you have enough space/facilities to house your target group?

"Grammy, why do you have to be so prepared?"

PK/4

- Grandpa's and grandma's house? Other?

- A vacation home, lake cabin, etc.?

- A motel/hotel with a pool?

We have used all three at different times, mostly associated with their age level and the unique needs at the time.

WHAT IS THE COST and how will this need be met?

With your co-director, research costs involved and set top-range costs to individuals considering the potential participants and what the families involved can afford. Get input for suggestions from the potential team member who could lead the crafts activity. Make choices or substitutions and adjustments to keep the cost in line. Have this information ready to share at your planning meeting.

NAILING DOWN THE DATE—the most difficult planning decision: Widen the scope and communicate with other potential participants for their input. You will remain flexible until most summer commitments take shape. Most churches and workplaces begin publishing dates and plans soon after the holidays: family vacations, company picnics, church youth camps, Vacation Bible Schools, school sports workout sessions, cheerleading camps, etc. The more kids the merrier—yes! But reality declares the more kids/families are involved, the fewer dates are available for all to participate.

By late February you can communicate your preferred two or three choices of dates to all parties. Suggest to them you need their input by March 31.

Communicate the date for a planning meeting early in April at this same time. Ask for an RSVP. Wait for a response. Nudge them if you don't hear back fairly soon.

Who? How Many?

The children?

Age distribution?

When the date is nailed down and communicated to all, it's time to see IF and HOW MUCH the families will be on board to support this project, since you can't do it by yourself. Call a planning meeting of all available adults. "Twenty-twenty" surely did teach us to use video conferencing, didn't it? That's surely a boon in this case! (Check for free options with ZOOM, WebEx, FaceTime, Skype, etc. Or perhaps one of your parents has their own subscription to one of these and can "host" the meeting.)

After that meeting, it's time to send letters and registration forms to the parents, and perhaps a flyer to the cousins for their bulletin boards. Set a due date for Registration forms and notarized "Permission to Seek Medical Treatment" forms to be returned. Check back with any that are tardy in this, since your Food Coordinator will need the information on allergies for planning purposes.

Remember, the number of children participating and their ages dictates how many adults MUST be on hand at all times to supervise. As parents, agree upon a ratio you are all comfortable with.

At your planning meeting discuss in quick fashion the jobs that MUST be done on site and then those that can be done off site before camp. Ask those in attendance to commit to a job at the meeting or get back with you as soon as possible.

The adults?

On-site availability?

Job Description

Individual jobs *may be* done by separate adult contributors but do not have to be. The point is that the following jobs must be done. So, to give opportunity for others to get involved, and for the sake of clear communication, we list them here as separate jobs.

Director: Gets the ball rolling by talking up "cousin camp" to the parents/adults. Enlists a co-director and heads up the planning.

Co-Director: Together they conduct the parents' meeting and delegate as much as possible to other parents, checking their progress regularly to coordinate all aspects of the cousin camp before, during, and after camp is done.

Food Coordinator: (Pre-camp: consults with Director/s to coordinate meal plans with the planned activities and any allergies noted on pre-registrations; purchase foods. On site: Directs use of the kitchen in food preparation, serving, and clean-up.)

Song Leader: (Pre-camp: Coordinates with Director/s to incorporate the camp theme and makes Song Sheets. On site: Leads singing.)

Craft Coordinator: Pre-camp: Coordinates with Director/s regarding choices and costs of crafts. On site: Directs afternoon Craft Time with assistance from all adults on hand.

T-Shirt design and acquisition Coordinator: Pre-camp: coordinates with Director/s on the color, design, sizes available and cost. Delivers t-shirts for Camp Council Meeting, first day of camp.

Bible Teacher: On site: Uses prepared materials in this Manual or develops their own.

First Aid & Safety Coordinator: Pre-camp: Assembles a well-stocked, easily transportable First Aid Kit. Checks expiration dates on contents. Makes sure First Aid Kit is at the site and on-board when the group travels to other sites. (This should probably be the Director or Co-Director. Someone who will be involved in every aspect of the going and doing of all the camp activities.)

How many other adult family members are willing and able to help with an at-camp contribution of time?

My daughter and daughter-in-law decided who came on Sunday and stayed until Tuesday noon. The other came back Tuesday noon and helped through Thursday's end-of-camp lunch that was prepared and served by the cousins.

A precious, valuable and sacrificial contribution for us came from a great-aunt and uncle who loved being with the kids, but who do not swim or get out in the sun. One of them made sandwiches and brought them to the beach for lunch. Then they sat with whistles in hand under an umbrella and watched the swimmers. They also served as mentors. They still feel a special bond to those children they worked with one-on-one at Cousin Camp.

> "Why do I have to be prepared? Because I've been unprepared before—I didn't like it." PK/14

Two more important questions: How? What?

THE CHILDREN WILL HELP! The cousins will love, or at least warm up to, being on a team and taking turns helping in the kitchen or at the campfire or picnic site—because you are making it fun.

Besides, it's part of the experience, part of the adventure to get to do BIG things. When younger, assign them to their tasks with adequate supervision and, if possible, pair an older cousin with a younger cousin to work together. (There is no greater bonding opportunity perhaps, than working together.) When older and more experienced, let them choose their tasks. Look for a sample Cousin Camp Kaper Chart printed in the Resource Section, p. 84 at the back of this manual.

You will need to watch how they work together. Why do two of them naturally chafe one another? Are they both in their realms "the smartest person in the room"? For whatever reason, vary your pairings so these two are not together in every task, but also don't avoid allowing them to learn to work together. It can be a great friend-making opportunity.

Oh, my, the possibilities of things to do at cousin camp are endless! You will consider no-cost resources at and near your site plus the ages and abilities of your children attending. If you can't get to a favorite activity this year, maybe next year! For a list of our springboard ideas—ideas that will turn on your lightbulb of inspiration and will make this project unique to you and your family, turn to p. 34 for Key Ingredient: Action Learning.

After Planning Meeting

CHECK LIST for Director/Co-Director

- Write a Form Letter and send to each potential Camper and their Parents.
  Include: An exciting flyer with all information for the camper's personal Bulletin Board with Date, Place, Theme, Major Activities. Request prayer for a successful and fun Cousin Camp.

- A Camper's Registration Form for each child that includes Contact Information for both Director and Co-Director during the Cousin Camp. Require on your Registration Form: Camper's information: Name, Age, T-shirt size, Birthday, Address, Allergies, Diet restrictions, Medications and specific instructions. PLUS: Both parents' contact information.

- A Note Requiring a notarized "Permission to Seek Medical Treatment" Form provided by the parent to be attached to Registration. (See the Suggested Link provided on p. 74. (When received, Registration and Permission Forms are to be filed in First Aid Kit.

- A Bring-To-Camp List that includes all items particular to your planned projects, e.g. dad's old t-shirt for a paint smock if you're planning to paint. See sample lists in Resource pages, p. 78.

- NOTE: If planning to make the video, p. 85, and involving the parents, you must communicate to the parents the time required to do so on the drop-off date. It requires approximately 1 hour and 15 minutes more time than a mere drop off. Also, casual clothes are needed.

A Key Consideration

The Cousins' Ages and Appropriate Safety Precautions

It is important to consider the ages of your cousins. Individually, of course, but your planning will also be affected by the average age of the children who will participate in any particular camp. In this regard, we discovered being flexible is a major requirement for the leaders who plan. Below are some generalities that describe the phases of cousin camps as we experienced them.

Q. What was the best thing about today? **A.** "Being outside all day." JA/5

Phase 1: "IT'S A BIG WORLD." In this introduction, most of the city cousins were being introduced to the greater outdoors. They are mostly pre-ten years old with some as young as three years old, if potty trained and with their mom. You can purchase Vacation Bible School type devotionals with age-appropriate activities around a common theme and Bible story. Short hikes, picnicking every day, swimming in a lake if possible, collecting rocks, learning to identify poison ivy, birdwatching, cooking together, craft time, kaper charts, campfires, camp songs, performing in a program on the last day. A quiet time in early afternoon and adequate rest are essential for the younger ones to enjoy their first experience away from home. (And perhaps for grammies to make it through the day!)

Phase 2: EXPLORATION PHASE: Cousins are mostly pre-teens, but the eleven-year-olds are already asking "Is cousin camp going to be too kiddish for me next year?" You will do many of the same things as before, but the cousins can make more choices,

Actual conversation:

Q. Grammy, how long are we going to have Cousin Camp?

A. As long as everyone wants to do it.

Q. What if one of us is going to college?

A. Wouldn't it be fun to go visit that college campus together?

take more responsibility, do more for themselves, be more creative. Your location/setting dictates some choices but change things up a little. Do early morning exercise to a kick boxing video, add tent camping and stargazing, with or without a telescope, plus all the old standby activities they loved. We added one-on-one mentoring for each child to have more time for one-on-one inter-personal communication. This age group can take on a major project with adult support but less supervision, such as acting out the story of Queen Esther in the Bible—complete with costumes, props, backdrops, etc.

Phase 3: NEW HORIZONS: Older swimmers are too old to swim at the lake with no lifeguard. (You might read that: Grammy and Grampa are too old to be lifeguards for kids who can swim so well.) Solution: Move back to our home in the city. Meet the first afternoon at the coolest place in town, an ice rink. Other days swim at a pool with a lifeguard, take a golf lesson early in the day or try indoor archery. At the house, the cousins did the cooking, and we added cooking contests. (One year, knowing the cooking contest was coming up, they were allowed to bring one secret ingredient, introducing intrigue into Cousin Camp.)

Plus, each family brought a parent-approved movie for the evenings. We volunteered at Shoes for Orphan Souls and went to a museum one year, the theatre another. This was generally a shorter cousin camp as the kids get busier and busier as they grow up.

Phase 4: "OFF TO SEE THE WIZARD" PHASE: The first one going to college became tour guide to show off her college campus and dormitory. We also explored the town, went to a movie, swam in the hotel pool, etc. We

"Playing golf at CC kind of laid the foundation for me to play golf for my high school team."
BA/17

had our devotional time on the hotel patio before heading out the next morning. (Our Cousin Camp adventure was shorter still—just one night away, but we were happy to find the only two days they all had available at the same time in the whole summer.)

Safety Precautions You MUST Have in Place.

- The address of the Cousin Camp site MUST be posted prominently in case of an emergency 911 call. The adults should enter the information in their cell phones.
- Parents should discuss and agree upon the ratio of kids to adults for all of Cousin Camp.
- A well-stocked First Aid Kit MUST be available wherever Cousin Camp goes. Check expiration dates annually. Designate an adult to tend to First Aid needs.
- A notarized Parental Permission Slip MUST accompany each child's registration for Cousin Camp with complete and current contact information for BOTH parents and MUST be in the First Aid Kit.
- Each child MUST wear their whistle on a lanyard at all times.
- No camper goes anywhere alone—always with a buddy.
- No camper wades in water/lake without swim shoes.
- Adult watchers MUST be on the beach watching, with whistles, during swim time.

"Grammy, I've been accepted to _____ University! I guess that means we know where we're going for CC this summer. JA/18

Key Element

A Coordinated Theme Throughout

After you've planned . . .

1) Your safety precautions such as fire extinguishers, life vests, posted address and 911 instructions at the site and have permission forms to seek emergency care if needed. See suggestions on p. 27.

> "That was a really cool experience ... getting to explore and kind of imagine what things had been like (for the U.S. Cavalry in the 1800s)."
>
> RN/16

2) AND REQUIRED the parents to provide a "Permission to Get Emergency Treatment" form for each child similar to the one seen at the link shown there.

3) Nutritious foods they will eat and how/who will prepare it, p. 79-83.

4) Adequate rest for all participants throughout the schedule.

5) Now you are ready to plan the.most.exciting.time of a kid's summer!

And that requires a coordinated theme throughout Cousin Camp. A catchy theme builds the excitement and deepens the impact.

INDIVIDUAL CAMP THEMES will come naturally out of the big picture activities you plan. Are you visiting a pioneer days fort? Your theme verse could be Psalm 59:16, "You are my fortress, my refuge in times of trouble." One of your menus can include a hobo stew cooked over a campfire, with each child adding one peeled and chopped vegetable or one canned item to the pot. (See the form for filling in your own original plans in the Resource Pages, p. 76.) Seek ideas from other parents, calling on their special talents, resources, and contacts.

YOUR CAMP T-SHIRT DESIGN could feature the motto "All for one & One for all!" There's a sample logo for your use on p. 32. Using and talking about this particular motto can combat a tendency for there to be factions within your group such as city cousins/country cousins or girls-against-boys. Your annual Cousin Camp T-shirt is actually a safety help in that when out and about you can keep track of them and they you even in a crowd by all wearing the same color shirt! Your wearing a hat also helps. (And when they outgrow their t-shirts perhaps you'll get a few of them back—to sew up the openings and make a colorful collection of Cousin Camp T-Shirt Pillows for your guest bedroom!)

> "Grammy, I get what you mean about being at the lake and thinking about the Bible story where you can't see any houses or cars or streets. You can imagine it all so much better there." BA/10

SPIRITUAL INPUT: You've bathed this project in prayer and enlisted the prayers of many. Now cousin camp is a perfect setting to practice Deuteronomy 6:7, "Talk about them [the theme verses, Bible stories, God's character, etc.] when you sit at home and when you walk along the road, when you lie down and when you get up."

Again, using age-appropriate Bible studies interspersed with a day of adventure and fun will surely cast a golden glow on the stories of ancient Bible characters and key verses learned.

Another year we assigned each child an adult mentor for the week. They had a short one-on-one Bible lesson. (Or two-on-one depending on your numbers.) The child chose the Bible story—all were different. (Suggestions are included in Ready-Made Plans included in this Manual.)

Each child met with their mentor after lunch (30 min.) and before Quiet Time (one hour). They read the passage together, or the Mentor read it and explained it. The Mentor

RN/5 yo asked for plaid shirts with buttons for back-to-school shopping— just like Uncle E's, his mentor at CC.

asked questions, defined words and described the setting. They worked together on memorizing a verse and praying. The Mentor helped the cousin put together a 1 to 3-minute presentation, e. g. a skit with props, for the end-of-camp program. (Oftentimes, the mentor became a character in the skit: Goliath for David's victory or a lion for Daniel's predicament.)

Here are some short notes on how we took advantage of our Cousin Camp setting when teaching the Bible lesson:

We added an Object Lesson and memory aid for a purchased curriculum on the Ten Commandments in Exodus 20. The cousins collected ten palm-size rocks on their hike and wrote Roman Numeral I – X on them. Then we played a game choosing a rock and looking up and reading or reciting the commandment.

One year we researched the actual/possible meaning of their names and assigned a positive message for their lives. We talked about the positive meaning of their names.

For in-town cousin camps we often had grandpa read a short passage and lead a discussion/share time. Some nights one of the older cousins gave an impromptu devotion or shared a testimony and led the discussion.

SINGING TOGETHER has a unique way of binding hearts together. A cousin theme song may ring in their hearts for weeks after camp too. It can carry over from one year to the next.

Only a few weeks ago, we received a text/video from a granddaughter singing our Cousin Camp theme song with her dog in a new kerchief—our own version of the chorus of the *Whiffenpoof Song,* "Rivet. Rivet. Rivet." (Frogs instead of sheep, for us!) "We're poor little [frogs] who have lost our way: "Rivet, rivet, rivet!" ….. "[Cousins at camp who si-ing off key.] Singing from here to . . . [please] have mercy . . . Rivet, Rivet, Rivet." Use your internet search engine or this URL: https://www.google.com/search?gs_ssp=eJzj4tFP1zcsNM0yMzJNzjZg9BIpyUhVKM_ITEtLzSvIz09TKM7PSwcAyYwL6g&q=the+whiffenpoof+song&rlz=1C1GCEA_enUS879US879&oq=The+&aqs=chrome.1.69i57j46j69i59j46l-

2j69i60j69i61j69i60.5596j0j7&sourceid=chrome&ie=UTF-8

Another favorite with adapted lyrics: "Creature Praise." We simply changed "creatures" to "cousins." Singalong: https://www.youtube.com/watch?v=1xhy38DCfU8 Lyrics: http://www.songlyrics.com/evie/creature-praise-lyrics/

Songs can serve practical purposes of bringing the group together, rousing their enthusiasm, or calming them down. Because of the complicated nature of reprinting them for you in this resource, we have opted instead to provide you the time-saving asset of URL links to the words and to YouTube performances to learn from. (If you are using a printed version of this Cousin Camp Manual, you can go to PeggyConsolver.com/cousincamp to access the Bibliography Listing of suggested URLs. In case a webpage is no longer active, please conduct your own search for a suitable alternative.

You undoubtedly have your own favorite songs, but here are a few of ours:

- **"I Am a Promise!"** https://www.youtube.com/watch?v=2dCvSafgCgw

- **"Oh, How He Loves You and Me!"**
  Music: https://www.youtube.com/watch?v=5D31_gjopSI
  Lyrics: https://gospelchoruses.wordpress.com/2016/01/10/o-how-he-loves-you-and-me/

- **"We've Got a Great Big Wonderful God!"**
  https://www.reverbnation.com/shannonsmith/song/8225024-weve-got-great-big-wonderful-god

- And a collection of songs with hand motions for kids! https://www.godtube.com/news/10-great-christian-songs-with-hand-motions-for-kids.html

ENJOY!

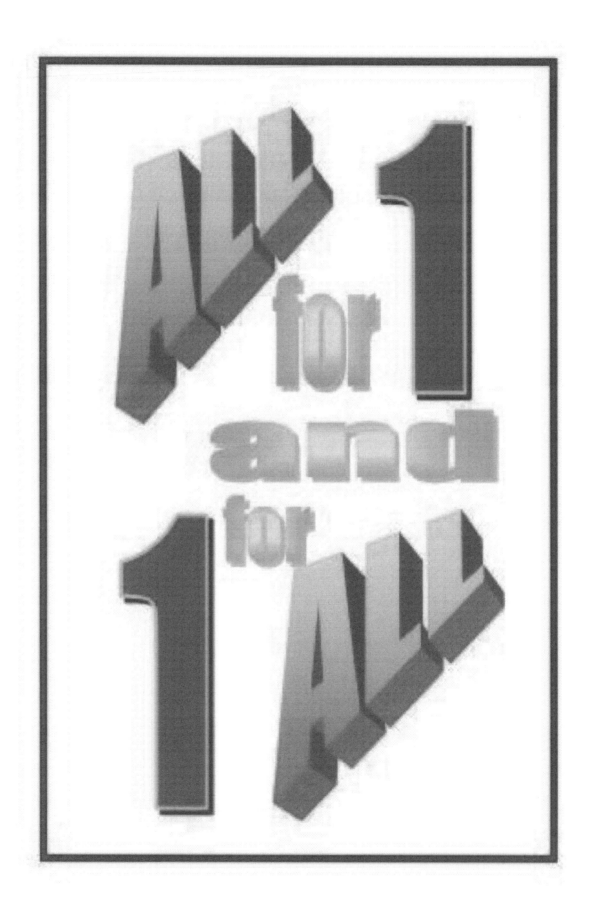

"O my **strength**,
I watch for You;
You, O God
Are my **fortress**,
My loving God."

–Psalm 59:9

The Key Ingredient
Action Learning

When all is said and done, it's hard to distinguish the Bible teaching that is saturated into the day's schedule of fun activities from the separate/not-so-separate topic of "action learning."

One example is using drama to teach the truths of Esther. Drama involves all cousins, all senses and all talents.

If they're older they can usually, with your help, take the drama to a far more creative cooperative effort than you expect. From the book of Esther, we told the exciting story and called on older cousins to read key verses from the Bible.

Cousins volunteered or were asked to play a part. Cousins made up costumes from a dress-up box.

Cousins built elements of the scene from large cardboard boxes. Cousins *played Esther* or rehearsed during Free Play Time.

Cousins performed the drama for parents at the program.

Cousins received praise for a great success, showcasing some unexpected talent!

The family videos and pictures will be enjoyed for years to come as they bring back the great memories of Cousin Camp.

And then, there's the one that got away. It taught us that not every plan works the way you imagined.

In 2011 two of our cousins returned from vacation with a fierce stomach bug that was contagious. Cousin Camp was cancelled. Ours being only two families of cousins meant if we followed through, we would have no cousins there. It would have been fun to carry plans through with grandparents and available grandchildren, but we think cancelling served a greater purpose of demonstrating our loyalty to one another: "All for One, and One for All."

Consequently, because that was our last year for camp at the lake, we have an unused original video script that you will find here in the Resource Pages, p. 85. Now years later, we plan to do a read-through as a "radio script" at our next family weekend at the lakehouse.

Blessings and fun to you and your family as you put together a silly episode with a ransom note, a "tall" monster, various "strange" characters at the lake, a music video on the beach, a strange encounter with pillow people who are NOT the enemy, etc. Your cousins will be presenting the world-wide premier of "Cousin Camp Mystery Theatre: 'The Strange Disappearance.'"

Adapt it to your Cousin Camp and ENJOY!

I'll say it again, the key ingredient to Cousin Camp which cannot be over-estimated is action learning. It's the adventure of discovery that lasts a lifetime.

The possibilities are endless, and HIGHLY ADAPTABLE—limited only by our imaginations. Here we provide a list of activities that will spark your imagination according to the resources available to you. These are things we did at Cousin Camps over the years.

At the Lake

The day Molly, the County Search & Rescue dog came to visit. Then there was: The year we built and launched rockets. And the day each grandchild first steered a vehicle sitting in Grammy's lap to drive the golf cart.

> Space Camp: "Oh-so-popular." CR

Hiking/Exploring	Swimming, wading
Visit a farm	Visit historic fort
Visit a power plant	Golf at driving range
Golf at putting green	Fishing & Picnics
Kick Boxing exercise video	Bird watching
Collecting fossils	Visited historic cemetery
Hiked abandoned railroad	Stargazing
Slept in a tent	Identify poison ivy
Built a campfire	

In-Town Field Trips Using Local Resources

Ice skating	Golf lesson	Archery lesson
Science museum	Natural history museum	Theatre production
Visit Cow Town	Zoo	Drive thru college campuses

When we swam at a neighborhood pool, we played basketball and dunked the ball through an improvised Swim Noodle Goal held up by Grammy or Grampa. (For several years Walgreen's has had a soft "hairy" beach ball in the spring that is so easy for all ages and sizes of hands to catch, grasp, and throw. (And it's so soft it does not hurt if it hits you.)

YOU HAVE TO EAT so engaging the kids in preparing simple meals is necessary action learning. A couple of years we had cooking contests and competed as Individuals (Best Burger/Slider) or Boys vs. Girls (Best Pasta Entre).

Essentially, Grammy is not interested in spending her whole time in the kitchen cooking and cleaning up. They had already been trained well at the lakehouse cousin camps so that by the time we transitioned to in-town they were good at all this. (I spend plenty of time in the kitchen at Thanksgiving.)

"It was cool because we all got to eat delicous food, and we all got to encourage each other and say, 'yeah, this was really good.'" BA

Couldn't resist this aside: "Now Christmas is another thing altogether! At our get-togethers the men and boys do all the cooking for "Christmas dinner" at the lakehouse on the weekend before Christmas. They cut/slice onions and peppers, stir in and heat pre-cooked Mexican Fajita meat from Sam's, fix Mexican Rice, make guacamole, heat tortillas, chop tomatoes and lettuce, put out grated cheese, sour cream, and salsa. It's been noted, we have nine (9) cutting boards/mats, etc. at the lakehouse, several paring knives, at least three potato peelers, etc. in a kitchen that definitely is NOT big, but there is a deck handy. And there you have our traditional Christmas feast! (Action Learning to the Rescue!)

Here are a few other action learning strategies we used:

To teach **GOOD NUTRITION** and the Five Food Groups, we encouraged wise eating habits at cousin camp. While making breakfast preparation easier with quicker clean-

Sunday School teacher to PK/4 yo: "What are these cute little things (embroidered fruit decals) on your dress, PK?"

"Food groups."

up, we hit upon the idea of self-serve, prepared items such as granola and nut bars, yogurt cups, fruits, toast w/peanut butter or w/cheese, and of course, milk and cereal.

Each child tried different combinations and tried to include as many food groups as possible in their breakfast from the large assortment of choices. We gave rewards or privileges and/or recognition to those who included the most food groups or tried new foods, etc.

They learned **CAMPING SKILLS** like how to build a campfire. Girl Scouts have a great teaching method for this by using snacks: mini marshmallows, red hots, pretzel sticks, coconut, etc. Google it. It's great.

EVEN QUIET TIME (QT) can have its action learning as long as they are in their assigned QT locations and quiet. ("Grammy needs a nap.") A small Library Shelf, with a variety of books: age levels from counting and learn-your-colors picture books to a storybook intro to Shakespeare. *The Case for Christ, Youth Version* by Lee Strobel. String Book for manipulating a loop of twine, etc.

"When I was a camp counsellor in Canada, I was the only one who knew how to lay a proper campfire." DK

A TAKE-HOME CRAFT will be a memento of a once-in-a-lifetime experience. When possible, your craft should be somehow related to the theme, theme verse, etc. Some suggestions: make plaster of Paris stepping-stones for their home gardens, paint with acrylics on a medium size canvas. [Be amazed which of the cousins takes to this project naturally.] A painted rock from Cousin Camp showed up in our 2020 Thanksgiving Scavenger Hunt on ZOOM!

Another year, we put handprints on a small pillow and made an abstract American flag on plain white canvas with all the cousins' handprints being in the stripes. Stars on the pre-painted blue field were five closely spaced index fingertips on each of fifty dots. To take home they "autographed" a plain pillowcase for each other.

Another time we asked a picture framer for scraps of matboard. Cut down at home

> "We (each family) contributed something to (our own family's) canvas and made a piece of (abstract) art (24x30) ... It hangs in my kitchen! A great memory." CA

into smaller pieces with a box opener, they can be great refrigerator magnets with camp logo, Bible verse, free-form original designs, etc. You can get peel-and-stick magnets at a crafts store.

Similar to that, you can ask at a local construction site if you can get some scraps of lumber. Paint a medium piece of 1x4 and hammer nails into it. Make a cross, or outline of a heart, etc. Attach a pull tab from a soft drink can on the back (before the hammering!) and voila, you have a unique wall hanging and memento from cousin camp! Or paint/draw directly on a discarded shingle or weathered fence board.

Visit your local craft store for lots of ideas with kits and materials and watch for sales. We've also done a composite family abstract in acrylic paints on a canvas frame for the lakehouse. Crafts stores also offer doorknob hangers for decorating and unpainted wooden treasure boxes.

OUTDOOR supervised Free Play Time for us included walking to the Bridgeview Store to buy ice cream bars and popsicles. That's action learning with a first taste of making a purchase on your own—pun intended.

Cousin Camp Is Nothing If Not Hands-On and Tactile.

NUMBER 1: Be outside as much as possible.

NUMBER 2: Be alert. Be watchful. Be safe.

NUMBER 3: Always have adequate adult helpers and whistles for all.

Be aware there are always risks. We MUST be prepared by *having BOTH parents' contact information with us at all times.* And annually having the parents sign a general liability release form with their child's registration and provide a Permission to Get Emergency Treatment Form for each child. Here is a link to a free source for these forms:

https://www.rocketlawyer.com/sem/release-of- liability.rl?id=154&partner-id=103&cid=1795580607&adgid=72188615952&loc_int=&loc_phys=9026 835&mt=b&ntwk=g&dv=c&adid=346362868225&kw=%2Bgeneral%20 %2Bliability%20%2Brelease%2 0%2Bform&adpos=&plc=&trgt=&trgtid=kwd-26581670945&gclid=Cj0KCQjw3ZX4BRDmARIsAFYh7ZIA7PpehHPJAFAqHwkgSA zRkDqyiulPWW0WDF

The Master Key

Discipline and Positive Motivation

There will always be at least a little conflict among individuals, perhaps both cousins and adults. So, how about a little positive motivation? Compliment Rocks defined below will point us all to looking for good behavior, noticing it, and showing public gratefulness for it.

If you want to take it a step further, you can have a cash-it-in system to use the rocks as currency to purchase "goods and services." Whether you have a stock of trinkets purchased for this purpose or privileges defined for a certain number of rocks or points, you will increase their desire to act appropriately or "wisely."

Compliment Rocks

BLUE for Encouragement:

GH - Great Helper!   WTG - Way to Go!

GJ - Good Job!   AP - Awesome Person!

RED for Love:

(Heart) - Love   ILY - I Like You

YS - You're Special   YAM - You Amaze Me

YELLOW for Appreciation:

TY - Thank You   GYF - I'm Glad You're Family

IAY - I Appreciate You

GREEN for Good Character:

ISGCIY – "I See God's Character In You"

-Humility

-Compassion   -Self-Control

-Love   -Gentleness

-Kindness   -Patience

Would you like a feather in your cap?

Used years earlier at Cub Scout Day Camp for a group of rowdy 2nd grade boys.

First Day: They were constantly putting each other down with unkind words and sarcasm.

Second Day: As everyone was required to wear a cap or hat, the leader stuck feathers from an orange feather duster in her hat for the second day. When asked why she had feathers in her hat, she said, "I'm going to give a feather for your hat as a reward to anyone I hear making a positive comment to someone else."

"What is a positive comment?"

"I'm glad you asked. It's a kind word or compliment or a nice thing to say."

On the last day, the leader had no feathers left in her hat. And when there was an unexpected 30-minute free play time in the schedule, her little group played nicely together because they had become friends, while other groups were rambunctious, playing chase and kicking each other and getting called down constantly.

An amazing result was seen another time in a **simple impromptu object lesson.** One young boy declined to join the small group activities. He followed at a distance as we explored a small creek. I spotted blood weed, a plant I was familiar with from my childhood on a farm. *Ambrosia trifida.* https://pfaf.org/user/Plant.aspx?Latin-Name=Ambrosia+trifida

Oh, yeah. Some people know it as giant ragweed.

I snapped a piece showing them the "blood" as its sap is red. I asked if they wanted to be "blood brothers." Then I made a small mark on each of their palms, saying, "Now you are all 'blood brothers.'" The loner joined the group as we went on exploring the creek.

You never know what will work, but the Lord will lead.

Another part of good discipline includes setting clear roles. You might want to designate parent/leaders as "captains" and "sergeants"—instead of Mommy/Daddy for the duration of the camp and require campers to address them as such. (This also fit the theme when going to a historic fort from the days of the U.S. Cavalry.)

It's important that other camp adults have authority to direct and correct any child at the point of incident. And for your child to come whining to you about it is a strict no-no.

As a result, your child will be freer to experience camp as the independent adventure it already is for the other children whose parents are not present.

Positive motivation to have fun, be safe, and treat others with respect is a subtle thing indeed. When you are successful, no one notices much. No one recalled any of it when interviewed. But without it, Cousin Camp would be a disaster with no one pleased about the experience.

Are they still friends years later? Do their eyes light up when Cousin Camp is mentioned? That's probably an indication that we were successfully using positive motivation. And as a result, everyone had fun. Everyone has positive memories that will last a lifetime.

The Basics

Camp Council Script, & Three Years of Ready-Made Wisdom Workout Plans

The Basics of Cousin Camp
Camp Council

Wisdom	Stature	Favor
1. Learn about God & Jesus.	1. Eat good food.	1. Respect others.
2. Learn about God's creation.	2. Exercise.	2. Use good manners.
3. Learn about history.	3. Get plenty of rest.	3. Be helpful.
4. Learning to make good decisions that please God.	4. Know safety rules.	4. Cooperate.
	5. Follow safety rules.	5. Have fun together.

7:00 Camp Council Meeting:

1. Introduce cousin songs to bring the cousins together. (See suggestions on pp. 30-31.)

2. Luke 2:52, Wisdom Workout is our Camp purpose and goal.

3. Prayer for this year's camp.

4. Introduce new theme and theme song.

5. Welcome and brief overview.

Camp Rules:

1. Nobody goes out alone.

2. Everyone wears his/her whistle during the day for emergencies. NEVER blow your whistle inside the house or car.

3. Everyone helps.

4. Everyone helps with camp kapers/jobs. (Decide on Team names whether birds, colors, etc. to fit your theme perhaps. Assign teams, Fill out Kaper Chart and Post it.) See p. 84. (Kaper teams for evening meals may at this time choose the entre for their

meal from menu options that have been planned.)

5. Everyone has a job to do, especially at mealtimes. Introduce adult lunch coordinator. Optional: Take food preferences for sandwiches, if this works for you. (Our lunch coordinator brought lunch to us at the swim beach/picnic site at 11:30 am. Other times we packed, a jar of peanut butter and squeeze jelly in a bag that stayed packed with tablecloth, etc., throughout cousin camp—ready to add fruit, chips, and a loaf of bread and "Grab & Go" for "a picnic" wherever we were going.)

6. Everyone wears closed-toe shoes outdoors—swim shoes in the water. (No one is allowed to get in the lake without swim shoes on.)

7. Everyone has his/her own backpack with water bottle and hat or cap and sunscreen and hand sanitizer and swim shoes at ALL outings.

8. Everyone takes care of his/her own things.

9. Everyone carries his/her own things.

10. Everyone keeps track of his/her own things.

11. Everyone helps one another.

12. Everyone gets a Cousin Camp T-shirt. Wear it on last day for the program. Put name on it. NOW. (Have black indelible marker available.)

13. Enlist older Cousin Helpers: (1 boy, 1 girl?) Helpers check the others to remind to bring backpack on every outing with water and water shoes and cap/hat, etc. Another helper may carry a bag of sit-upons on hikes. Etc.

14. Check the Kaper Chart before bedtime. Which Kaper Teams have Breakfast?

Early Morning Schedule

Explain the schedule is general and flexible, but it is good to have the first day be kind of low-key and on-schedule to start out—since they had a hard time going to sleep the first night of Cousin Camp!

No one is out of their room before 7 am except for going to the bathroom.

You may dress and put your pajamas in your bedroll. You may make your bed or bedroll.

You may, one at a time, go to the bathroom and brush your teeth. You may put away your things for the day. (Visual check.)

You may help someone younger.

If not done before 7:00, these things MUST be done before Devotions/8:30.

At 7:00 Kaper Team _____ assembles at the kitchen to do breakfast kapers. (Check the Kaper Chart.)

At 7:30 Eat breakfast together.

At 8:00 Kaper Team _____Cleans Up.
OTHERS Prepare for Devotions. Bring your Bible.

(LEARN MORE TOMORROW.)

(IF THERE'S TIME IN THE SCHEDULE BEFORE "Evening Devotional" Play a game like "Twister" or "Button, Button. Who's Got the Button," or "Fruit Basket Upset." (Include a bathroom break.)

First Evening Schedule

At 8:00 Evening Devotional: (Transition and bring together w/Cousin Song) Adult: Share your Heritage Story (Example: A story about your common heritage, about the history of the family, or about an individual great-grandpa, great-grandma and the positive character that their life illustrated, etc.)

At 8:30 Twilight Songs: Soft songs, slow songs, praise songs.
Share time/questions: Kaper Chart Check.
One more song. (Slow and soft) Prayer. Goodnight!

At 9:00 Bedtime routine. Brush teeth.

At 9:30 Must be in bed or bedroll. (If not sooner!)

At 10:00 Lights out.

Wisdom Workout #1

Age Level: "It's a Big Wonderful World" Phase

Theme for Cousin Camp:
"It's a Big Wonderful World!"

Cousin Camp Bible Verse:
"For You created my inmost being; you knit me together in my mother's womb. I praise You because I am fearfully and wonderfully made."
Psalm 139:13-14

Introduce Theme Song:
"We've Got a Great Big Wonderful God"
https://www.reverbnation.com/shannonsmith/song/
8225024-weve-got-great-big-wonderful- god
Adapt words for a second verse: "He made a great big wonderful world!"

Truth to Live By:
"God knows me and loves me."

Craft Resources

Plenty of easy crafts to make from your hiking-and-collecting nature adventures: https://www.pinterest.ca/JeweledRose/nature-kids/

Plenty more ideas, perhaps a little more advanced: https://www.pinterest.ca/suzietoots/nature-ideas/

Here are exciting activities/crafts that will spark creativity and learning opportunities: https://www.pinterest.ca/booknblues/connecting-kids-to-nature/

Something for everyone: https://www.pinterest.ca/jvanthul/nature-art-for-kids/

```
..................................................
:                                                :
:   GROUP PROJECT:                               :
:        Campfire Dinner                         :
:          Sing Along                            :
:                                                :
..................................................
```

Major Activities of This Cousin Camp

(To add to the fun, leaders might assume the titles of Captain and Sergeants to avoid calling the leadership mama and aunt so-and-so, etc.) During all activities, one adult helper is taking a few notes of the adventure. At the end of the day, note-taker will write up a short narrative of the high points. Cousins will pantomine for program.

First Afternoon/Night: Swimming, Dinner & Camp Council

DAY 1: (At Morning Devotions or at Lunch, assign Mentors & Mentees for QT later.) Take an easy hike along a country road, Learning & Collecting. Swimming, Picnic, Quiet Time.

Craft Time: Use collected items from hike for art.

Snack Time: Learn Fire Safety: "How-to-Build-a-Campfire."

Free Play, Dinner, Evening Devotions, Sing-Along and Games.

DAY 2: Morning Devotion. Easy hike in a wooded area if available. Watching for Wildlife & Identifying what you're seeing. End at the site chosen for the evening campfire if possible. Explore the area. Return to Swim area, Picnic, Quiet Time, Craft Time. CC Big Project: Cookout Weiner Roast, Game Time, Sing-Along and Evening Devotion.

DAY 3: After Morning Devotions, Field Trip to a nearby farm if possible, Swimming, Picnic, Quiet Time, Craft Time. Dinner, Twilight Hike. (Use flashlights for safety at dusk.) Watch the Sun go down; Evening Devotional. Listen for Night Sounds and identify, Stargazing, Sing-Along and Games. (How about "Wanna Go on a Bear Hunt?" at the house?)

DAY 4: Program for Parents: Include Individual and Group presentations "Adventures at Cousin Camp." Narrator reads down the schedule calling out an item: 'We brushed our teeth'/Cousins pantomime the action, plus one or two other regular items. "The favorite thing of that day was": *(Cousins' choice.) Repeat for each day at camp.*

Program Finale: "Cousin's Bear Hunt" https://scoutermom.com/16172/going-bear-hunt/

Cousins serve lunch to parents/guests first.

DAILY MORNING ROUTINE

No one is out of their room before 7 am except for going to the bathroom.
- You may dress and put your pajamas in your bedroll. You may make your bed or bedroll.
- You may, one at a time, go to the bathroom and brush your teeth. You may put away your things for the day.
- Help someone younger.
- If not done before 7:00, these things MUST be done before Devotions at 8:30.*

At 7:00 Kaper Team _____ assembles at the kitchen to do breakfast kapers. (Check the Kaper Chart.)

At 7:30 Eat breakfast together.

At 8:00 Kaper Team _____ Cleans Up.
OTHERS Prepare for Devotions. Bring your Bible.

At 8:15 Assemble with Bible.
Sing/Teach: Cousin Songs, action songs, camp songs, praise songs, CC Theme Song.

At 8:30 CC Theme Verse from open Bibles.
Devotion for the Day.

At 8:40   Prayer for the day's activities:
Announcement of plans for the day:
Special Assignments:
Special Instructions:

At 8:50   Break to Assemble with needed gear. (Sing Cousin Song to signal assembly.)
(When appropriate, sing to assemble, as you travel in car, as you hike, as you do Kapers, etc.)

9:00   Begin Major Planned Activities of the Day
It's a Big Wonderful World!
God knows me and loves me!

DAILY AFTERNOON ROUTINE

1:00-1:30   QUIET TIME WISDOM WORKOUT with Mentor: (See choices and suggestions, p. 54.

1:30-2:30   REST TIME ALONE: (Check out a book or other QT resources from Camp Library. Read a book, Draw/Sketch, Write in Notebook or Journal, String game, Sleep).

2:30-3:00   Transition to Craft Time, Craft Set-Up, Kaper Team _____ helps set up.

3:00-4:00   CRAFT TIME & SNACK TIME (Day 1, Teach "How to Build a Campfire." With pretzel sticks, marshmallows. . . https://cubscoutideas.com/3385/learn-campfire-safety-with-a-craft-edible-campfire/)

4:00-4:30   DAILY HOUSEKEEPING KAPERS, see Kaper Chart, p. 84.

4:30-6:00   Late Afternoon: Supervised FLEX TIME play

5:30-6:00   DINNER PREPARATION (Kaper Team _____)

6:00-6:30   DINNER SERVED

6:30-7:00   DINNER CLEAN UP (Kaper Team _____)

7:00   Planned Evening Activity

8:00	Evening Devotional: Adult: Share something from your Common Heritage about the history of the family, or an individual great-grandpa, great-grandma and the positive character that their life illustrated, etc.
8:30	Twilight Songs: Soft songs, slow songs, praise songs. Share time: "What was the best thing about today?" (Take notes, include in program.) Kaper Chart Check for tomorrow.
9:00	Bedtime. Brush teeth.
9:30	Must be in bed or bedroll. (If not sooner!)
10:00	Lights out.

WISDOM WORKOUT #1
Morning Devotionals

CC Theme Verse: *"For You created my inmost being; you knit me together in my mother's womb. I praise You because I am fearfully and wonderfully made."* Psalm 139:13-14

WISDOM WORKOUTS: "It's A Big Wonderful World!"

Day 1: When you say this verse, you are saying the truth: "God knows me. He made me. With great care and tenderness." You were not an accident or a mistake in any way. Be thankful that God knows you. That means God knows what you need. And he gives you what you need. Let's thank God that He knows us, and loves us, and takes care of us.

WISDOM WORKOUTS: "It's A Big Wonderful World!"

Day 2: Did you notice as we hiked along we saw all kinds of plants and flowers and trees? Did you learn the names of some of them? You know, just like God made you, He made every one of them. Just like He knows you, He knows all about them too. Everyone is special—even the poison ivy. Why would God make poison ivy? Maybe it was to teach us wisdom. To see if we would be wise and not touch something that is not good for us. To see if we will honor God and obey. Let's thank God that we are learning to be wise this week.

WISDOM WORKOUTS: "It's A Big Wonderful World!"

Day 3: Did you see the stars come out last night as the sun was going down? Did you know God made every one of them too? And He has a name for every one of them. He set them each one in its special place just so. So, the Moon goes through a new cycle of changes every 28 days. And the earth turns on its axis once every 24 hours. And the Earth circles around the Sun once every year. Ev-er-y year. Is that amazing or what?

God surely did make a Big Wonderful World! Let's thank God that He made this big wonderful world, and He made us and put us in just the right place in His world.

WISDOM WORKOUT #1
Mentor Sessions

Individual Bible Study Choices:

"Abraham & Son Isaac on Mt. Moriah," Genesis 22:1-18

"A Wife for Isaac," Genesis 24

"Jacob's Dream at Bethel," Genesis 28:10-22

"Joseph in Prison," Genesis 39:19-23 and 40:1-23

"Moses as a Baby," Exodus 1:22-2:10

"Moses and the Burning Bush," Exodus 3:1-17

"Mary & Martha, Friends of Jesus," Luke 10:38-42 and/or John 11:17-44

DAY 1: Read the story in the Bible with your adult helper/mentor.

Talk about what you read. Who are the main characters? How old do you think they are in the story? On paper provided by Mentor, draw a picture of some part of the story.

DAY 2: Read the story in the Bible again with your adult helper/mentor. Retell the story in your own words.

What is God teaching you in this story?

Add more detail of this story to the picture you began yesterday.

DAY 3: Read the story in the Bible with your adult helper/mentor one more time.

This week we are learning 3 main things: 1) that God made you and loves you, 2) He wants us to know Him, and 3) He wants us to praise Him.

Does this story illustrate one of those points?

How can you share this story with others? Finish your drawing and explain it. Write a story. Do a pantomime. Write a song. Tell what you learned for your own life. Dress up as a character in the story and tell his/her part of the story. Or make a larger drawing of the story to share with all. Etc.

Be prepared to share this at your program on Day 4.

Wisdom Workout #2

Age Level: Exploration/Space Camp

Theme for Cousin Camp:

"Space Camp!"

Cousin Camp Bible Verse:

*"Trust in the Lord with all your heart and lean not
on your own understanding; in all your ways acknowledge
Him and He will make your paths straight."*
Proverbs 3:5 & 6

Introduce Theme Song:

"The Countdown Song" by Dorothy Montgomery
Words: https://gospelchoruses.wordpress.com/2014/12/01/somewhere-in-outer-space/
YouTube: https://www.youtube.com/watch?v=Krlp5Tan4dU

Truth to Live By:

"God will direct my path."

Craft and Science Resources

Pinterest has lots of ideas for crafts and activities with a space theme: https://www.pinterest.ca/pin/138767232251156879/

Science for Kids website with experiments and fun science activities will take this theme to a whole new level: https://www.science-sparks.com/diy-space-camp/

This source touts "simple ideas with profound results" for a space theme summer camp: https://www.mymundaneandmiraculouslife.com/diy-sensory-summer-camp-space-theme/

GROUP PROJECT:
Make your own rocket.
Launch your own rocket.
See a bigger re-usable rocket launch demonstrated, if possible.

Perhaps one of your resources will be a talented parent who will take a day of paid time off to join the fun and lead in this most exciting adventure of Cousin Camp . . . ever! His/her child will be so proud! (Or perhaps a local hobby rocketeer will supply the demo of a bigger re-usable rocket.)

This website and source explains how it works: https://estesrockets.com/get-started/ And "with equal emphasis on providing safe and exhilarating learning experiences" their website provided this standardized pledge of safety standards for hobby rocketeers: https://www.nar.org/safety-information/model-rocket-safety-code/ which made us feel better about recommending what Uncle E. our resident rocketeer and 6th grade science teacher helped us with one year.

Major Activities Of This Cousin Camp

First Afternoon/Night: Swimming, Dinner & Camp Council, Evening Devotionals.

DAY 1: Morning Devotionals, Space Camp Learning and Doing, Swimming, Picnic, Quiet Time, Craft Time, Flex Time, Campfire Dinner & Cousins begin writing our "Moon Adventure at Cousins Camp," Stargazing, Camp Out in Tents, Evening Devotionals.

DAY 2: Morning Devotionals, Space Camp Learning and Doing, Swimming, Picnic, Quiet Time, Craft Time, Flex Time, Night-Time Hike, Stargazing, Cousins write another chapter of "Moon Adventure at Cousins Camp," Evening Devotionals.

DAY 3: Morning Devotionals, Space Camp with Rocket Launch, Swimming, Picnic, Quiet Time, Craft Time, Flex Time, after dinner Cousins write last chapter of "Moon Adventure at Cousins Camp," Evening Devotionals.

DAY 4: Space Camp Program for Parents: Include Individual and Group presentations. Program Finale: Cousin narrator/s read original short story of "Moon Adventure at Cousins Camp" with others acting it out in pantomime.

Cousins serve lunch to parents/guests first.

Daily Morning Routine

No one is out of their room before 7 am except for going to the bathroom.
- You may dress and put your pajamas in your bedroll. You may make your bed or bedroll.
- You may, one at a time, go to the bathroom and brush your teeth. You may put away your things for the day.
- Help someone younger.
- If not done before 7:00, these things MUST be done before Devotions at 8:30.*

At 7:00   Kaper Team _____ assembles at the kitchen to do breakfast kapers. (Check the Kaper Chart.)

At 7:30   Eat breakfast together.

At 8:00   Kaper Team _____ Cleans Up.
OTHERS Prepare for Devotions. Bring your Bible.

At 8:15 Assemble with Bible.

Sing/Teach: Cousin Songs, action songs, camp songs, praise songs, CC Theme Song: "Somewhere in Outer Space."

At 8:30 CC Theme Verse and Devotion for the Day.

At 8:40 Prayer for the day's activities:

Announcement of plans for the day:

Special Assignments:

Special Instructions:

At 8:50 Break to Assemble with needed gear. (Sing Cousin Song to signal assembly.) (When appropriate, sing to assemble, as you travel in car, as you hike, as you do Kapers, etc.)

9:00 Begin Major Planned Activities of the Day

Space Camp "God will direct my path."

Daily Afternoon Routine

1:00-1:30 QUIET TIME WISDOM WORKOUT with Mentor

1:30-2:30 REST TIME ALONE: (Check out a book or other QT resources from Camp Library. Read a book, Draw/Sketch, Write in Notebook or Journal, String game, Sleep).

2:30-3:00 Transition to Craft Time, Craft Set-Up, Kaper Team _____.

3:00-4:00 CRAFT TIME

4:00-4:30 DAILY HOUSEKEEPING KAPERS, Kaper Team _____.

4:30-6:00 Supervised SNACK TIME & FLEX TIME outside.

5:30-6:00 DINNER PREPARATION (Kaper Team _____.)

6:00-6:30 DINNER SERVED

6:30-7:00 DINNER CLEAN UP (Kaper Team _____.)

7:00 Planned Evening Activity

8:00	Evening Devotional: Adult: Share something from your Common Heritage about the history of the family, or an individual great-grandpa, great-grandma and the positive character that their life illustrated, etc.
8:30	Twilight Songs: Soft songs, slow songs, praise songs. Share time: "What was the best thing about today?" Kaper Chart Check.
9:00	Bedtime. Brush teeth.
9:30	Must be in bed or bedroll. (If not sooner!)
10:00	Lights out.

WISDOM WORKOUT #2
Morning Devotionals

> **CC Theme Verse:** *"Trust in the Lord with all your heart and lean not on your own understanding; in all your ways acknowledge Him and He will make your paths straight."*
> Proverbs 3:5 & 6

WISDOM WORKOUTS: "Space Camp Wisdom: God Will Direct My Path"

Day 1: Have you ever thought about being a pioneer? Someone who explores unknown territory? Maybe like the Pilgrims who came to Massachusetts and founded what became the United States of America. Or maybe someone who studies previously unknown things like tiny little germs and viruses we can't even see to find out how they grow and how we live with them. Or have you thought about becoming an astronaut and going to the Moon? Or Mars? Wow, the more we learn, the more we see how much more there is to learn! Because there is so much to do and so much to learn, we need to trust God who knows all about all of it. Let's thank God we can count on Him to direct our path.

WISDOM WORKOUTS: "Space Camp Wisdom: God Will Direct My Path"

Day 2: Have you ever met a know-it-all? Someone who thinks he or she knows everything? They wave their hands to answer every question the teacher asks. If you're excited about doing something new, they think that's old-stuff. They've already done that and they're on to something way bigger. Do they know about tomorrow? They may act like they do, but they don't. But God does. In fact, He knows all your tomorrows—right now—way before you have any idea about it.

Let's thank God who knows about all our tomorrows, and that we can trust Him to direct our path—every day. One by one. (Introduce song: "Why Worry When You Can Pray?")

WISDOM WORKOUTS: "Space Camp Wisdom: God Will Direct My Path"

Day 3: Trust. What is trust? Would you trust a chair with a broken leg? Would you trust a bus that's going the wrong way or has a flat wheel? Would you trust a person who breaks promises over and over? Do you know who you can trust? . . . God never breaks a promise. God loves you. He wants you to know Him. God wants you to trust Him. And He will direct your life. If you want to know more about how to trust Him, talk to me or to your mentor during Quiet Time today.

WISDOM WORKOUT #2
Mentor Sessions

Individual Bible Study Choices:
Choose a verse or verses from below or draw out of a hat.

John 3:16, God wants me to trust Him.

1 Samuel 15:1-29, Saul chooses his own wisdom.

Psalm 23:1-4, The Lord is my Shepherd.

Psalm 23:5-6, The Lord knows all about the enemy.

2 Chronicles 1, Solomon asked for wisdom above power & riches.

Daniel Chapters 1 and 3, The Lord will help me.

Acts 9:1-19, God got Saul's attention and redirected his path.

DAY 1: Read the story in the Bible with your adult helper/Mentor.
Talk about what you read. Who has power in this verse? Who are the characters? What is the main point of this verse or verses? With paper provided by your Mentor, draw a picture of some part of this verse or passage.

DAY 2: Read the story in the Bible again with your adult helper/Mentor.
Retell the verse/story in your own words. What is God teaching you in this verse/story?

DAY 3: Read the verse/story in the Bible with your adult helper/mentor one more time. This week we are learning 3 main things: 1) that God wants us to know Him, 2) He wants us to believe in Him, and 3) He wants us to know He has a plan for us. Does this story illustrate one of those points?

How can you share this story with others? Write a story. Do a pantomime. Write a song. Tell what you learned for your own life. Dress up as a character in the story and tell his/her part of the story. Make a larger drawing of the story to share with all, etc. Be prepared to share this at our program on Day 4.

Wisdom Workout #3
New Horizon Phase

Theme for Cousin Camp:
"God's Power in My Life"

Cousin Camp Bible Verse:
*"Finally, be strong in the Lord and in His mighty power.
(11) Put on the full armor of God so that you can take
your stand against the devil's schemes. . . (13) Therefore put
on the full armor of God, so that when the day of evil comes, you
may be able to stand your ground."*
Ephesians 6:10-13

Introduce Theme Song:
"Victory in Jesus," Eugene Monroe Bartlett
Words:https://www.google.com/search?q=song%3A+Victory+in+Jesus&rlz=1C1GCEA_
enUS879US879&oq=song%3A+Victory+in+Jesus&aqs=chrome..69i57j69i58.11554j0j4&-
sourceid=chrome&ie=UTF-8

Truth to Live By:
"God is For me."

Resources

Art: https://www.youtube.com/watch?v=EotjL8ncUXM

Name Art: https://www.pinterest.ca/search/pins/?q=name%20art&rs=typed&term_meta[]=name%7Ctyped&term_meta[]=art% 7Ctyped

Science: The Basics of Science Through Experiments: https://frugalfun4boys.com/awesome- electricity-projects-for-kids/

Make your own electricity: from a stack of coins? . . . from a potato? . . . https://www.sciencebuddies.org/science-fair-projects/project-ideas/energy-power

There's a whole world to explore . . . in electricity: https://www.pinterest.ca/pin/572731277597835090/

GROUP PROJECT:

Make a video, (re-printable script provided to modify, or write your own)

"The Cousin Camp Mystery Theatre: The Strange Disappearance" Imbed video shoots into the regular schedule of Cousin Camp.

(This will require a minimum of editing of the video to be shown at the Parents' Program.)

Major Activities Of This Cousin Camp

OPTIONAL: "Cousin Camp Mystery Theatre," See complete Goofy Script in Resource Section. (Before parents leave on drop-off day, make Video Scenes 1 & all segments of 2. Requires about 1:15.)

First Afternoon/Night: Swimming (Make a Music Video at the Beach of the Frogs' Rivet Song (or your cousin song), Dinner & Camp Council, and Evening Devotions.

(PLANNING NOTE: Make T-shirts purple, if possible, to coordinate with video OR change color of sash in script.)

DAY 1: Power Camp: Learning and Doing. (Video: Sc3, Ransom Note; Sc4, Old Tree/ Hiker; Sc5, Fisherman) Swimming, Picnic, Quiet Time, Craft Time (Make "Pillow People" Costumes), Campfire Dinner & Rehearse next segments of video, Stargazing, Camp Out in Tents. (Or not! Your choice.)

DAY 2: Power Camp: Learning and Doing, Swimming, Picnic, Quiet Time, Craft Time, Flex Time, Night-Time Hike, Stargazing, (Video: Sc6, Birdwatcher; midday at beach, Sc7, music video of Cousin Song; Scary early twilight video, Sc8, Pillow People.)

DAY 3: Power Camp: Field Trip to an electrical power plant, if possible, or to your local power provider. Swimming, Picnic, Quiet Time, Craft Time, Flex Time, After Dinner Make the last segments of "The Cousin Camp Mystery"; Sc9: Old Hag; Sc10, Fork in the Road. Any extras needed. (Minimum editing to put Sc 2, Parents Rescued at the end. And Music Video in Middle.)

DAY 4: Power Camp Program for Parents: Include individual and group presentations, songs and skits. End with "world premiere of 'Cousin Camp Mystery Theatre: 'The Strange Disappearance.'"
    Cousins serve lunch to parents/guests first.

Daily Morning Routine

No one is out of their room before 7 am except for going to the bathroom.
  - You may dress and put your pajamas in your bedroll. You may make your bed or bedroll.
  - You may, one at a time, go to the bathroom and brush your teeth. You may put away your things for the day.
  - Help someone younger.
  - If not done before 7:00, these things MUST be done before Devotions at 8:30.*

At 7:00   Kaper Team _____ assembles at the kitchen to do breakfast kapers. (Check the Kaper Chart.)

At 7:30   Eat breakfast together.

At 8:00   Kaper Team _____ Cleans Up
OTHERS Prepare for Devotions. Bring your Bible.

At 8:15   Assemble with Bible.
Sing/Teach: Cousin Songs, action songs, camp songs, praise songs, CC Theme Song. (Is there a cousin to lead one or more songs?)

At 8:30   CC Theme Verse and Devotion for the Day.

At 8:40   Prayer for the day's activities:
Announcement of plans for the day:
Special Assignments:
Special Instructions:

At 8:50   Break to Assemble with needed gear. (Sing Cousin Song to signal assembly.) (When appropriate, sing to assemble, as you travel in car, as you hike, as you do Kapers, etc.)

9:00   Begin Major Planned Activities of the Day

Power Camp: Learning about electricity with simple science experiments. Also, safety with electrical appliances. (Give opportunity to wash clothes without a washer and dryer. It might prove useful sometime! Also, an exercise in gratefulness. Like when we dug with archaeologists in Israel!)

Daily Afternoon Routine

1:00-1:30   QUIET TIME WISDOM WORKOUT with Mentor

1:30-2:30   REST TIME ALONE: (Check out a book or other QT resources from Camp Library. Read a book, Draw/Sketch, Write in Notebook or Journal, String game, Sleep).

2:30-3:00   Transition to Craft Time, Craft Set-Up, Kaper Team _____.

3:00-4:00   CRAFT TIME & SNACK TIME (Personalize "Pillow Case Face" if making the video.)

4:00-4:30   DAILY HOUSEKEEPING KAPERS, Kaper Team _____

4:30-6:00   Late Afternoon: Supervised FLEX TIME play

5:30-6:00   DINNER PREPARATION (Kaper Team _____)

6:00-6:30   DINNER SERVED

6:30-7:00   DINNER CLEAN UP (Kaper Team _____)

7:00   Planned Evening Activity

8:00   Evening Devotional:
Adult: Share something from your Common Heritage about the history of the family, or an individual great-grandpa, great-grandma and the positive character that their life illustrated, etc.

8:30   Twilight Songs: Soft songs, slow songs, praise songs.
Share time: "What was the best thing about today?" Kaper Chart Check.

9:00   Bedtime. Brush teeth.

9:30   Must be in bed or bedroll. (If not sooner!)

10:00   Lights out.

WISDOM WORKOUT #3
Morning Devotionals

CC Theme Verse: *"Finally, be strong in the Lord and in His mighty power. (11) Put on the full armor of God so that you can take your stand against the devil's schemes... (13)..., so that when the day of evil comes, you may be able to stand your ground."* Ephesians 6:10-13

WISDOM WORKOUTS: "Power Camp Wisdom: "God Is For Me."

Day 1: Here at Cousin Camp we've always liked our walking stick. We use it to walk along with confidence. It can save us from a stumble. It can test the depth of the water. We could use it to fight off a mean dog. Would you choose a walking stick that bends? Or is too short? Or is not strong enough? God wants you to trust in Him and be strong in His mighty power. Will He bend or break? Is He too far away to help you? Is He stronger than the enemy? The first piece of God's armor He wants you to have is His belt of Truth. You can know Truth through His Word. He wants you to put it on. Read it. Wear it. It will make you wise and with it you can stand strong. Just like this stick, too weak to be a walking stick. It's made strong when you pair it with an iron bar. Remember, God is FOR you. You and God are an unbeatable pair.

WISDOM WORKOUTS: "Power Camp Wisdom: "God Is For Me."

Day 2: How is your heart? God's Word uses the heart as the place of our emotions and our hidden thoughts. How are you doing with that? Are you quick to be angry? Envious? Afraid? God offers you today a "breastplate of righteousness." It will protect your heart. It's not something you can do for yourself. It's easy to be angry. It's impossible to not be angry about many things—if you don't have God's righteousness as your armor. This armor is actually a free gift. Jesus paid for it when He died on a cross for your sins 2,000 years ago. Would you like to put on that free gift today? Talk to me or your mentor now or at Quiet Time. Remember, God is FOR you.

WISDOM WORKOUTS: "Power Camp Wisdom: "God Is For Me.""

Day 3: The armor of God also includes the shield of faith, the helmet of salvation, and the sword of the Spirit. If you've accepted the free gift of righteousness through Jesus, you have this shield of faith that protects you from lies and deception. The helmet too protects your head and keeps you from falling into temptation. Your strongest weapon is the Sword of God's Spirit which is His Word. One of the truths is: He will never leave you nor forsake you. Put on God's armor. I hope you'll do that today. Talk to me or your mentor at Quiet Time. Remember what? God is FOR you.

WISDOM WORKOUT #3
Mentor Sessions

Wisdom Workout, Individual Choices:

**Joseph, The Outsider: Genesis 37:12-36 & 50:12-21,
power to forgive and not hold a grudge.**

Samson, the Strong Man: Judges 14-16, power to overcome pride.

Gideon, the General: Judges 6:11-7:25, power to overcome fear.

Deborah, the Judge: Judges 4:1-23 & 5:4, 6, 20-21, power to lead.

Mary, Mother of Jesus: Luke 1:26-56, power to do God's will.

Zacchaeus, Tax Man: Luke 18:18-42, 19:1-9, power to do what's right.

Peter, Disciple: Acts 10:1-48, power to obey.

DAY 1: Read the story in the Bible with your Mentor. Talk about what you read. Who are the main characters? How old do you think they are in the story? On paper provided by your Mentor, draw a picture of some part of the story. Or describe this main character in your own words and how you think he feels.

DAY 2: Read the story in the Bible with your Mentor again. Retell the story in your own words. What is God teaching you in this story? Add more to your picture on the back of this page. Or more to your description.

DAY 3: Read the story in the Bible with your mentor one more time. This week we are learning 3 main things: 1) That all power comes from God, 2) How to have God's power in our lives, 3) What to do to overcome peer pressure. How does this story illustrate one of those points?

How can you share this story with others? Suggestions: Write a story. Do a pantomime. Write a song. Tell what you learned for your own life. Dress up as a character in the story and tell his/her part of the story. Read your description. Share the story through your art, etc. Be prepared to share at our program on Day 4.

Resources:

Bibliography of Internet Links

Planning Summary Form

Letter to Parents Checklist

Bring-to-Camp List

Breakfast Choices

Menu Suggestions

Sample Kaper Chart

Bibliography

NOTE TO THE USER: Whether you are working from a hardcopy edition OR from a digital version, if any of these links are inactive, please go to PeggyConsolver.com and click on "Cousin Camp Manual/ Bibliography. These internet links will be tested periodically by the author and suitable substitute links provided. ENJOY THE ADVENTURE OF COUSIN CAMP!

Foreword, p. 7:

Brooks, David. "The Nuclear Family Was a Mistake," *The Atlantic Daily*, . https://www.theatlantic.com/magazine/archive/2020/03/the-nuclear-family-was-a- mistake/605536/

"DAVID BROOKS is a contributing writer at The Atlantic and a columnist for *The New York Times*. He is the author of *The Road to Character* and *The Second Mountain: The Quest for a Moral Life*."

Joyner, D. "7 Reasons Why Cousins Are The Most Important Part Of The Family Unit," BLAVITY: NEWS, July 5, 2017, Accessed June 4, 2021. https://www.blavity.com/cousins?-category1=blavityreads .

Singing Together, pp. 30-31:

"The Whiffenpoof Song," Lyricist: Pomeroy, George S., 1910. Accessed June 4, 2021. https://www.google.com/search?gs_ssp=eJzj4tFP1zcsNM0yMzJNzjZg9BIpyUhVKM_ ITEtLzS vIz09TKM7PSwcAyYwL6g&q=the+whiffenpoof+song&rlz=1C1GCEA_enU-S879US879&oq= The+&aqs=chrome.1.69i57j46j69i59j46l2j69i60j69i61j69i60.5596j0j7 &sourceid=chrome&ie=U TF-8.

"Creature Praise," Accessed June 4, 2021. Karlsson, Evelyn Tornquist, [Evie]. Accessed June 4, 2021. Lyrics: http://www.songlyrics.com/evie/creature-praise-lyrics/. Singalong: https://www.youtube.com/watch?v=1xhy38DCfU8

"I Am a Promise," Gaither, Gloria, 1979. Accessed June 4, 2021. https://www.youtube.com/watch?v=2dCvSafgCgw.

"Oh, How He Loves You and Me," Kaiser, Kurt, 1975. Accessed June 4, 2021. Music: https://www.youtube.com/watch?v=5D31_gjopSI , Lyrics: https://gospelchoruses. wordpress.com/2016/01/10/o-how-he-loves-you-and-me/.

"We've Got a Great Big Wonderful God" Spencer, Tim, 1963. Lyrics and Music: https://www.reverbnation.com/shannonsmith/song/8225024-weve-got-great-big-wonderful-god

A collection of Top 10 Christian songs with hand motions: https://www.godtube. com/news/10- great-christian-songs-with-hand-motions-for-kids.html

Concerning Risk, p, 38-39:

"Release of Liability," Rocket Lawyer at RocketLawyer.com. Accessed June 4, 2021. https://www.rocketlawyer.com/sem/release-of- liability.rl?id=154&partner-id=103&cid=1795580607&adgid=72188615952&loc_int=&loc_phys =9026835&mt=b&ntwk=g&dv=c&adid=346362868225&kw=%2Bgeneral%20 %2Bliability%20%2Brelease%20%2Bform&adpos=&plc=&trgt=&trgtid=kwd-26581670945&gclid=Cj0KCQjw3ZX4BRDmARIsAFYh7ZIA7PpehHPJAFAqHwkg-SAzRkDq yiulPWW0WDFQfNjw7NjMT_5w7pp4aAjbgEALw_wcB#/

Wisdom Workout #1, God's World, p. 49:

Nature Crafts Suggestions, p. 49: https://www.pinterest.ca/JeweledRose/nature-kids/ https://www.pinterest.ca/suzietoots/nature-ideas/ https://www.pinterest.ca/booknblues/connecting-kids-to-nature/ https://www.pinterest.ca/jvanthul/nature-art-for-kids/

Program Suggestion, p. 50: https://scoutermom.com/16172/going-bear-hunt/

"How to Build Campfire" Snack suggestion, p. 51: https://cubscoutideas.com/3385/ learn-campfire-safety-with-a-craft-edible-campfire/

Wisdom Workout, #2, Space Camp, p. 56:

Suggestions for Crafts, Experiments, Activities:
https://www.pinterest.ca/pin/138767232251156879/
https://www.science-sparks.com/diy-space-camp/
https://www.mymundaneandmiraculouslife.com/diy-sensory-summer-camp-space-theme/
https://spaceplace.nasa.gov/

Hobby Rocket resources, p. 56:
https://estesrockets.com/get-started/
https://www.nar.org/safety-information/model-rocket-safety-code/

Wisdom Workout, #3: "God's Power in My Life," p. 63

Theme Song, p. 63: Bartlett, Eugene, 1885. "Victory in Jesus." https://www.google.com/search?q=song%3A+Victory+in+Jesus&rlz=1C1GCEA_enUS879US879&oq=song%3A+Victory+in+Jesus&aqs=chrome..69i57j69i58.11554j0j4&sourceid=chrome&ie=UTF-8

Resource suggestions, p. 64:

Name Art:
https://www.youtube.com/watch?v=EotjL8ncUXM
https://www.pinterest.ca/search/pins/?q=name%20art&rs=typed&term_meta[]=name%7Ctyped &term_meta[]=art%7Ctyped

Science experiments:
https://frugalfun4boys.com/awesome-electricity-projects-for-kids/
https://www.sciencebuddies.org/science-fair-projects/project-ideas/energy-power
https://www.pinterest.ca/pin/572731277597835090/

Planning Summary Form

When? & How Long? _____

Where? _____

What? _____
(Major Activities=Expenses, Theme)

How Much? _____

Adults Available: _____

Children: _____

Age Distribution? _____

Letter to Parents Checklist

(Set your Required Return Date by consulting with the food coordinator and camp t-shirt coordinator and as to how much time they need before camp.)

A. **Letter**. Announcing Dates, Place, Major Activities and Contact Information for Director/Co-Director, Required Return Date of registration forms. (Mention allergy information needed to plan menus.)

B. **Registration Form.** To be returned by (Insert date.) for each child should include:
      1) Full information for one child,
      2) Specifics regarding any medications and food allergies.
      3) Contact information for both parents.

C. **Notarized Permission Slip** (provided by parent/s) for each child, for use in case of emergency. Parents return with Registration by date required. (Suggested Link included on p. 74.) (File returned forms in First Aid Kit.)

D. **Separate T-shirt order form including size options and cousin's name**. (Parents return with Registration by date required.)

E. **B**ring-to-Camp List: Include all items particular to your special projects, e.g. old t-shirt for paint smock. (Sample: p. 78.)

NOTE: If planning to make the video involving the parents in the first scene, you must communicate to the parents the time required to do so on the drop-off date. It requires about 1:15 of their time, and they will need to wear casual clothes. AND add "Old pillow case" to Bring-to-Camp List for each cousin.

Bring-to-Camp List

(ALL items marked with camper's name)

- CAMPER'S INFORMATION FORM, (1 for each child) Including:
  Contact information (for both parents: cell, home, email) Health Information:
  Allergies, Medications/Instructions, etc.
  Permission Slip, notarized (for getting emergency treatment if needed) (See
  suggested link, p. 74.)

- Whistle on a cord or lanyard
  Flashlight

- Closed-toe shoes and socks at all times outdoors

- Swim shoes, at all times wading or swimming in lake

- Backpack: (With you at all times in either personal backpack or on your belt): water
  bottle hand sanitizer
  - hat or cap   sunscreen
  - tissue pack   small insect repellent
  - pocket change for a cold snack (if a small store is available)

- Sleeping bag

- Personal items in week-ender size bag, including:
  - 1 pair long pants   Tops & bottoms for each day
  - Toothbrush, toiletries   Hairbrush, etc.
  - Underwear   Pajamas

- A carpet sample or similar size carpet scrap for a sit-upon

- Paint shirt (Dad's old t-shirt?)

Breakfast Choices

Grain Group

Cereal

Oatmeal

Bread/toast

Bagel

Tortilla

Vegetable Group

Potatoes, hash browns

Tomato, slice or juice

Picante sauce

or Lettuce, Spinach

Peppers/onions for omelet

Any other available

Fruit Group

Applesauce

Banana

Cantaloupe

Oranges

Blueberries, frozen for Smoothie

Strawberries, frozen, for Smoothie

Dried apricots, cranberries, raisins

Any other available

Milk Group

Milk, plain or flavored

Cheese: American slice or grated

Mozzarella stick or grated Cottage

Cheese Yogurt

Cream cheese

Meat Group

(Contains Protein)

Canadian Bacon Or Ham

Peanut Butter

Walnuts

Almonds

Eggs, boiled

Eggs, to cook

Egg Substitute

Refried Beans

Bacon

Menu Suggestions 1st Night & Day 1

DINNER:

Maybe Fried Chicken Carry-Out?

Dessert: Prepared ahead: Cake

BREAKFAST CHOICES p. 79

LUNCH/Picnic:

"Grab & Go" Sandwiches, OR Made-to-Order Sandwiches

Add before take-off: Loaf of bread, chips, fruit, drinks, new trash bag.

"GRAB & GO" PICNIC BAG: Always in the bag: plastic tablecloth, Clorox wipes, han-di-wipes/hand sanitizer, trash bag, cutting board, paring knife, paper towels for napkins, Peanut Butter, squeeze jelly. (NOTE: Always wipe tablecloth with Clorox wipes before folding and returning to bag=ready for the next time.)

DINNER SUGGESTIONS #1, Choices for Kaper Team _____:

SPAGHETTI & MEATBALLS: Meatballs, spaghetti, spaghetti sauce, Parmesan OR

STROGANOFF & MEATBALLS: Meatballs, medium egg noodles, onion, mushroom soup, paprika, sour cream or plain yogurt. Look into a crockpot recipe for this item. It might come in handy in case you have an outing scheduled. Kaper Team can prepare in Crock Pot before leaving=slow cooking magic!

SALAD: Garden Salad or Pea Salad

VEGETABLE: Steamed Broccoli or Roasted Veggies

DESSERT CHOICE: (Instant Pudding or Canned fruit) & Cookie

Menu Suggestions Day 2

BREAKFAST CHOICES p. 79

LUNCH/Picnic p.

DINNER #2, Choices for Kaper Team _____:

JAMBALAYA W/GR. BEEF OR GR. TURKEY (Pre-cooked/frozen): Jambalaya Mix, Cooked ground meat. OR Check for Crock Pot recipes if it would fit your schedule of activities better.

BURRITOS W/GR. BEEF OR TURKEY (Pre-cooked): Tortillas, Cooked ground meat, Taco seasoning packet, Tomatoes, Lettuce, Grated Cheese

GO-WITHS: Canned green beans and/or corn, Refried Beans, etc.

SALAD: Cantaloupe or Watermelon

DESSERT CHOICE: (Instant Pudding or Canned fruit) & Cookie

Menu Suggestions Day 3

BREAKFAST CHOICES p. 79

LUNCH/Picnic p.

DINNER #3, Choices for Kaper Team _____:

BAKED POTATO W/CHILI (OR pre-cooked chopped brisket): grated Cheese, Plain Yogurt or Sour Cream OR

SALMON CROQUETS: Canned Salmon, cracker crumbs, eggs, chopped onion

STEAMED RICE

VEGETABLE: Steamed Broccoli or canned or frozen Peas & Carrots mix.

DESSERT CHOICE: (Instant Pudding or Canned fruit) & Cookie

Substitute Weiner Roast Menu:

Hot dogs & Condiments:

Go-Withs: Cheese, Relish, K/M, Buns, Onions,

Pork 'n Beans or Ranch Beans, Cantaloupe/Watermelon

DESSERT: S'Mores: Marshmallows, Chocolate, Graham Crackers

Menu Suggestions Day 4

BREAKFAST CHOICES p. 79

LUNCH FOR PARENTS:

PREPARATION TEAM: Kaper Team _____ (After Breakfast)
CLEAN-UP TEAM: Kaper Team _____ (Housekeeping)

LASAGNE

BROWN & SERVE ROLLS

GARDEN SALAD

DESSERT: Cupcakes & Icing

Sample Kaper Chart

Date:

DAILY:	DAY 1	DAY 2	DAY 3	DAY 4
Make bed/roll up Sleeping bag	All	All	All	All
Breakfast Teams:				
Get Ready				
Clean Up				
Brush teeth, dress (dirty clothes in Individual laundry bags)	All	All	All	All
Lunch Teams:				
Get Ready				
Clean Up				
Quiet Time Rest	All	All	All	All
Housekeeping Daily:				
Sweep kitchen:	Boys	Girls	Boys	Girls
Empty trash,				
Replace bags:				
OR				
Tidy Bathrooms:				
Tidy Common Area:				
Vacuum/Dust				
Supper Menu Choice				
Get Ready				
Clean Up				
Shower/Teeth/Bed	All	All	All	All
Kaper Chart Check Up	All	All	All	All

Cousin Camp Mystery Theatre

"The Strange Disappearance"

In this lighthearted spoof, Your Cousins rescue their parents!

Parents unwittingly have walked into a trap and are kidnapped by a "tall" monster. (Where were their whistles?) Relentless (mostly) in their search, Cousins range far and wide (sort of) and meet many interesting local characters while searching. (Though they probably took time out to do "Snack Time" and "Swim Time.") "Sit back and enjoy the world wide premier of Cousin Camp Mystery Theatre presenting "The Strange Disappearance."

(Compliments of Peggy Miracle Consolver, Author)

Scene 1: The Strange Disappearance

Location: _____ Time: _____

SLUGLINE: Exterior, Sunshine/Open area, large tree/in frame, left

SHOT FROM LADDER: Opens with parents/distance, right frame/strolling to nearer left, but not toward tree in frame.

(Script Walk-Thru)

PARENTS: (middle ground in frame/nearer old oak tree) *(Ad lib. small talk)*

MOMS: "What a beautiful morning."

"It's a perfect day."

DADS: "The kids were so tired they're still sleeping."

"I wonder if the fish are biting."

(Parents drawing nearer.)

(SOUND EFFECTS: *a branch snaps near camera for big noise)*

PARENTS: *(React/Fear)* THEY HEAR.

THEY STOP.

THEY TURN. *(To tree and camera)*

THEY LOOK UP.

THEY GASP IN FEAR! *(and FREEZE!)*

CAMERA: GOES BLACK. (5 sec.) *(Clear scene.)*

(Quiet on the set! From the top, Take 1!)

CAMERA ON: (NOT on ladder, FOCUSES on a purple sash hanging from a Branch.) SWAYING IN THE BREEZE.

CUT!

Change locations. . . . .
Prepare for Scene 2!
Move quickly!

PROPS Cousin: Ladder, Small Branch, 1½-2" X 4' (breakable) Purple Sash

PERSONNEL:

CAMERA Adult, use ladder (make Monster's eye-view seem taller though not seen)

(No cousins in scene. Quiet! Only on sidelines.)

Parents, in old/Casual clothes we can tear. (Clothes torn in next scene.)

Cousin SOUND Person: Step on (to break) branch on cue, NEAR CAMERA FOR MAXIMUM SOUND.

((Cousin PROPS Person: SAVE 2 pieces of BRANCH for Scene 4.))

(CAMERA: Leaving space for splicing later.)

Cousin PROPS Person: Tie long purple sash in branch after parents gasp when, camera off. (BRING ladder.)

[Final Edit: Splice in here "Sc3a-3b and on" for continuing action.]

Purple sash

MOVE TO NEXT SCENE:
Cousins prepare parents' MAKEUP as HOSTAGES.

DIRECTOR'S NOTES:

SCHEDULE: Scene Must be done BEFORE Parents leave from Dropping off cousins.

Communicate Time required for Video Shoot to parents BEFORE they arrive IN LETTER TO PARENTS. Bring old shirt we can tear/Sc 2. TOTAL Estimated/Time Required: 1:15 minimum.

Asst. Dir: Script person BEFORE THE SHOOT: (Review script. Adjust. Esp. Sc. 1-2c.)

CONSULT/CONFIRM with: Camera person & Location scout. All scenes.

CAMERA PERSON: Please consider saving each scene after filming, or at end of day to a computer to avoid accidental deleting of completed scenes.

Scene 2: Parents Are Hostages!

Location: _____ Time: _____

(*Make up: Gruesome after battle with monster.*)

(Script Walk-Thru)

SLUGLINE: EXT., not in sunshine, somewhere "deep in the woods"

SHOT: close-up/parent, most ghastly, huddled with others

(Pan out)

ALL LOST PARENTS: (*tattered, mutilated, Writhing in pain, weak*) *Tied up together WITH PURPLE SASH.*

PARENTS: ALL (*ad lib*):
"Help! (*weakly*) Help!"
"Who can help us?"
"Oh-h-h." (*moaning*)
"I feel faint."
"Which way did he go?"
"Is anyone out there?"
"Will anyone ever find us?"

OFF CAMERA: (*COUSINS TO THE RESCUE!*)

COUSINS: (Singing IN THE DISTANCE: "Rivet Song")
Cousins sing off-camera, coming closer, closer . . . slowly . . .
"Rivet Song"
"We're poor little frogs who have lost our parents! Rivet   Rivet   Rivet!.

(*CAMERA ON PARENTS . . . ROLLING . . . NO BREAK IN ACTION*)

PARENTS: (*Tied up, languishing.*)
"What was that?"
"Sssh! Listen!
"It's singing" . . . .

continue to Scene 2a

Props Person: BRINGS: 2 pcs of Branch, Song Sheets, Sound Effect instruments, Scissors, long Purple Sash
AND. . .

Make-Up Kit and *Smock/Bib/each*
Lotion such as Jergen's
Mousse for hair. And/or gel.
Hay straw, dried grass.
Red lipstick, optional Ketchup.
Black eyeliner. Dark eye shadow.
Cream/lotion to remove make up.

MAKE-UP EFFECT:
Gruesome, dirty, w/dried grass in hair on end, tangled
Ripped clothing, open wounds, bruises, arm hangs limp

Make up session: 5 min. QUICKLY:
Parents: Choose make-up smock.
Apply lotion.
Kids make up their parents:
(Then each other, minor smudges.
Cousins need:
Only a small amount of MAKE-UP
Minor dirt smudges (eye shadow) on cheek, brow, or chin)

(Cousins change to new purple CC T-shirts.)

SCRIPT Person: HO/PU Scripts
BEFORE V-shoot. Leads the
WALK-THRU 2, 2a, 2b, 2c.
[*Editor will splice in intervening Scenes made during CC.*]

DIRECTOR'S NOTES:

IN LETTER, Before they arrive:

Ask parents' permission to "make them up" for a video that will be taped during Cousin Camp. Shown at program.

Ask them to bring their own lotion and make-up remover if they wish.

Their scenes will be "A Strange Disappearance"

And "Cousins to the Rescue"

TIME ESTIMATE:

Move/new locale:	10
--Make-up	10
--Set-up & Walk-Thru	5
--Video shoot	10
TOTAL	**25 min.**

((Sc 2, 2a, 2b, 2c will be spliced to the end and will be The End.))

Scene 2a: Cousins to the Rescue (...Continuing fr/Sc2)

SHOT: CAMERA STAYS ON PARENTS

(Parents' faces . . . from agony to hope.)

COUSINS: (OFF CAMERA: Singing in the distance. Coming closer, slowly.)

PARENTS: *(Add more dialogue if there are more parents.)*

"Kids?" . . .

"Our kids!"

"They're coming here!"

"Can they help us?"

ON-SET EXTRAS: *(Off-camera: Growling, "Who goes there?" . . . lots more growling!)*

COUSINS: (OFF-CAMERA: Singing STOPS in the distance.)

SHOT: CAMERA STAYS ON PARENTS

COUSINS: (STILL OFF CAMERA) *ALL: ad lib*

"The monsters!" . . .   "The real monsters!" . . .

"They're really tall!" . . .   "But we can beat them!" . . .

"We must—for our parents!"   . . .

"All For One and One For All!" . . .

COUSINS: *(Repeat: together)* "All for One and One for All"

PARENTS: (All) GASP . . . *(fear returns!)*

"They're so little."

(SOUND EFFECTS BEGIN . . . . . Bonk . . . wham . . . whop . . .

COUSINS: "You mean ole Monster!"

Bonk!   Bam!   Bop!

Clank!   Whoof!

"Take that you cad!"

Bonk!   Bam!   Bop!

Clank!   Whoof!

One Parent (CLOSE UP):   "But mighty in spirit."

. . . . *continuing from Scene 2.*

PROPS, ETC.:
Song Sheets

SOUND EFFECTS INSTRUMENTS:
Percussion
wooden spoons,
Small cardboard boxes,
Plastic swim pool,
Garbage can lid,
Plastic baseball bats,
Golf bag,
Broom, etc. . . . .

(Continue to Scene 2b...)

DIRECTOR'S NOTES:

Scene 2b: Battle & Climax (...Continuing Scene 2)

(Camera Rolling! ... No break in Action!) (HIGH-energy scene!)

SHOT: *(ON PARENTS: dodging, flinching, cringing at battle sounds)*
(CAMERA: STAYS ON PARENTS UNTIL: "CRASH/SILENCE"

SOUND EFFECTS . . . Continuing! *. . . Continuing! Fierce Battle . . . in progress . . .*

COUSINS: *(OFF CAMERA: Sound Effects Person-3, Dialogue-2, or more)*

    C1 : "How dare you kidnap our parents!

        Bonk! Bam! Bop!

        Clank! Whoof!

    C2 : We'll teach you for messin' with our family!

        Bonk! Bam! Bop!

        Clank! Whoof!

(OFF-CAMERA: **Continuous to CRESCENDO!**
All instruments in a "drum roll.")

(LOUDER!   LOUDEST!   DRUMROLL!   BAM!)

C-R-A-S-H!   *(SILENCE!!)*

CAMERA ON PARENTS, still.

CAMERA GOES BLACK:

          ....   **CUT!**

Same props from Scene 2a:

(COUSINS OFF-CAMERA)

--ALL COUSINS: Making Sound Effects in quick succession.

--2 COUSINS: (C1 & C2) Insert Dialogue among sound effects.

Asst. Dir. Directs:

--Crescendo: ALL COUSINS work the sound-makers in a Drum-roll, continuous/faster.

--LOUDER!
--LOUDEST!
--DRUMROLL!
--BAM!

(CLIMAX)
SILENCE!!

((ALL COUSINS wearing CCTee For next scene!))

((Minor skirmish Make-Up for next scene, if not done already.))

DIRECTOR'S NOTES:

Registration and Check- in Note:

COUSINS RECEIVE T-SHIRTS ON ARRIVAL, (Label it immediately.) Take to V-shoot.

TIME ESTIMATE: 5 MIN.

Scene 2b: Est. Time: 5 min

Scene 2c: Denouement (...Continuing from Scene 2b)

Break if needed. (MAKE-UP: if not done before in Sc2.)
DIALOGUE WALK-THRU

SHOT: *Cousins Approaching: (Marching feistily w/backpacks.)*
(Singing Reprise: last part of "Cousins" Song as Cousins enter Frame Wearing Purple CC T-shirts with backpacks, MINOR SIGNS OF A BATTLE.)

COUSINS: *Untie parents. Give water bottles. Continue Singing:*

". . ."Cousins at camp who sing off-key,
Searching from here to eternity.
Please have mercy on such as we.
Rivet   Rivet   Rivet!"

COUSINS & PARENTS together: *(Add more dialogue if you have more parents.)*

ALL COUSINS:

C3: "Mom, Dad, are you all right?
ALL PARENTS: "We are now!" "You are our heroes!"
"Thanks, guys!" "What happened to you guys?"
C4: "It's a long story!"
C5: "Mommy, are you hurt?"
I'll be okay."
C2: "Dad, you look awful!"
"What? You don't like my new do?"
P4: "How did you find us?"

SHOT: *(Close-Up):* SMALLEST COUSIN:
C5 : "You would NOT believe it." *(Puts on Purple Headband—NOT Same one wearing P/H before.)*

SHOT: (Widens out) *Smallest cousin FRONT, wide stance, fists on hips.*

OTHER COUSINS BEHIND: *Arms locked.*

CUT!   IT'S A WRAP!

                    Editor adds: THE END

MAKE-UP! *5-min (Should be done in Sc2. If not, here.)*
Cousins carry backpack. Carry baseball bat, tennis racket, walking stick, wooden spoon etc. like a weapon though they used it as a percussion instrument.

PREPARE FOR SCENE
Minor smudges On cheek,
Chin, Forehead

PROPS:
First Aid Kit, Backpacks
Water bottles, extra

VIDEO EDITOR:
Add "The End" and
Credits to Disguised Cousins

--Old Hag
--Old Fisher
--Hiker
--Sunbather
--Artist
--Birdwatcher
--Tennis Player
--Hunter
--Basketball Player, etc., more strange characters if more cousins

Add at Beginning:
Title:
<Cousins Camp 20__ Presents>
Cousin Camp Mystery Theatre: "The Strange Disappearance"

DIRECTOR'S NOTES:

CAMERA PERSON:
Please consider downloading each scene after filming, or at end of day to a computer to avoid accidental deleting of completed scenes.

NOTE: First Aid Kit (FAK) is in every outdoor scene.
Carried by a different Cousin in each scene.

PURPLE HEAD BAND:
-Not same person each scene.
-Each scene has punchline w/ wearer of PHB.
-cover PHB w/hat or wig if also the DC/Disguised Cousin in in that scene. (Remove hat/ wig for the PHB punchline.)
-Sc9, PHB is DC/ "old hag."

Scene 3a: Breakfast, Day 1   Time:_____

SLUGLINE: Interior, morning at CC, breakfast set-up

SHOT: Open with close-up of "Food Group" choices. Pan out to Take in Cousins choosing, fixing breakfast, sitting down to eat on deck, etc.

DIALOGUE WALK-THRU: *Ad lib while self-serving breakfast.*
Someone is humming Cousin Camp Song/Rivet, Rivet, Rivet. . . Ends w/several joining in for the Chorus: "Cousins at Camp. . .
(C3: finds RANSOM NOTE. Impaled on a screwdriver, Wedged in a crack or such. . .)

COUSINS: C3: "What's this?"
            C2: "Let's see."
            C1: "Read it."
            C3: "'We have your parents. Bring $5,000 to the old Oak Tree.
            . . tonight at sunset, or ELSE!' Signed . . . "The Monsters""

COUSINS: *(Confused talking all at once)*
            C5: "Oh no! Where are my mommy and daddy?"
            C2: "Our parents have been kidnapped?!"
            C3: "Oh no! What can we do?"
            C1: "I thought they went Home."
            C4: "We don't have 5 grand!"

SHOT: *(Close-up, Cousin wearing Purple Headband. (PHB))*
            C2: "We have to save them!" *(Older Cousin/wearing PHB. Calm/de-termined.)*

                    . . . continues in Scene 3b:

PROPS Person: (Assemble props needed/return props.)

Food Groups poster

Breakfast, regular set-up

Screwdriver

Ransom Note: "We have your parents. Bring $5,000 to the old oak Tree . . . tonight at sunset. . . OR ELSE!" "The Monsters"

Script Person: *HO/PU Scripts*
BEFORE V-shoot. Leads "Dialogue Walk-Thru."

One older cousin wears a Purple Headband.

DIRECTOR'S NOTES:

(In CC Schedule:
--at breakfast Day 1)

TIME ESTIMATE:
15 min.

Scene 3b: Breakfast, Day 1

Scene 3 continued:

DIALOGUE WALK-THROUGH:

VARIOUS COUSINS: *(Excited. Worried. Thinking. Looking around.*
Suspicious. Ad lib. Random order OK.)

  "Let's go find them!"

: "Where? They could be anywhere!"

: "Wait, guys. Calm down! We have to make a plan!"

: "Yeah, we need a plan."

: "Where were they last seen?"

: *(PHB looks straight at camera:)* "We should start at the old oak tree.
Maybe we'll find a clue there."

: "Everybody get your backpack and your water bottle and meet back
here in ten minutes ready to go look for them."

: "Good idea."

: "I'll get the First Aid kit. They may be hurt."

: "Hurry guys! We're on a mission to save our parents!"

: "I hope my mommy and daddy are okay!"

CAMERA: *(Close-up on Cousin with PHB.)*

: "I wonder who could be behind this?"

    . . . .   CUT!

(NEXT SCENE 4: at the oak tree)

PROPS, ETC.:
First Aid Kit,

Purple Headband (PHB)

CAMERA PERSON: Please
consider downloading each scene after
filming, or at end of day to a computer
to avoid accidental deleting of completed scenes.

FAK: first aid kit

Purple headband.

DIRECTOR'S NOTES:

TIME ESTIMATE:
--Make-up   0
--Set-up   5
--Run throughs 10
--Video shoots 10
TOTAL   25 min.

Scene 4: Old Hiker at the Oak Tree/First Clue

SLUGLINE: EXT., oak tree: Location: _____   Time: _____

DIALOGUE WALK-THROUGH:

SHOT: Opens in Wide view, cousins enter (Right) in the distance.

(Purple Sash, not seen yet, hanging outside left frame/close up.)

(Cousin 1 carries the First Aid kit. (DC: Cousin at rear of Line averts face, hat worn low, (disguise-ready).

SHOT: (action) medium view down, of feet as Cousins draw nearer

COUSINS: *(Go all around the tree looking for clues—on the ground.)*

(Last Cousin drops out, completes disguise, enters (Left) on cue.)

SHOT: *(Steps back and purple sash is in frame, hanging.) Zooms to Medium close in, looking mostly at feet/ground.*

COUSINS: *(Ad lib.)* "Do you see any clues?"

"No. Do you?"

"Does this mean anything?" (pointing to broken branch)

"Maybe."

SHOT: pans out/Purple Sash/L. frame/DISGUISED COUSIN: *(Enters Left)*

COUSINS: "Look! Here comes someone!"

"Maybe she/he will know where our parents are!"

"Yeah, let's ask her/him."

"Hello. Have you seen our parents?"

DC "Old Hiker": *(in strange voice/character):* "What do they look like?"

COUSINS: "My dad has really short hair and sideburns."

"My mom has brownish-red hair. Sometimes."

"My dad has black hair."

"My mom has curly blonde hair, most of the time."

(ADD DIALOGUE AS YOU SEE FIT.)

DC: "Nope. Haven't seen them. Why don't you look at the beach?" *(Cousins nod.)*

SHOT: Close-up/Cousin w/PHB.

PHB COUSIN: Starts to say something. . . shrugs.

PROPS: Backpacks, FAK, Last Cousin's disguise, Small branch/broken, purple sash & ladder.

Props Person:

Hang purple sash from tree.
Place Broken Branch, 2 pieces.

Action:

Cousins HIKING *(Enter Right)* with backpacks. In Line. Water bottles on Belt.

First Cousin: Carries Large Old Suitcase marked with red tape to indicate "First Aid."

Co-Dir: in charge of Disguised Cousin, (DC), last Cousin becomes "Disguised Cousin" in each scene.

((Pick DC the night before and have costume consultation.))

MAKE UP: Last Cousin's disguise partially done b/f hiking in, but hides face, looks other way, etc.

*Add: **Wig? Change hat? Garish lipstick? Etc.***

DIRECTOR'S NOTES:

For safety sake: Download video each day.

TIME ESTIMATE:
-- Make-up   0
-- Set-up   5
-- Run throughs 10
-- Video shoots 10
   TOTAL   25 min.

Scene 5a: On the Beach (Reader)

Location: _____ Time: _____

SLUGLINE: EXT., beach, (Stand near "Reader" for distance, then close-up)

DIALOGUE WALK THROUGH:

SHOT: Wide view on All Cousins

COUSINS: *(Approaching along the beach. No. 1/First Aid kit.; last/becomes Disguised Cousin.)*

C1: "Hello. Have you seen our parents?" *(Quick off/on to set up DC)*

SHOT: CLOSE-UP: DC sitting, reading, *(War & Peace)* etc.
Widens to take in Cousins questioning Reader on the Beach.

DC: *(in character/voice)* : "What do they look like?"

COUSINS: "My dad has a mole on his forehead and my mom has brown eyes.
: "My dad has brown eyes.
: "My mother has a big mouth. . .the biggest in her class in Sixth Grade." *(Add dialogue as needed.)*

DC: *(in character, thinks a moment)* : "Hmmm, Interesting. But I do not believe I have encountered such interesting people today. Have you looked at the boat dock?"

COUSINS: *(ALL: Turning to go.)* Good idea!. . .Thanks!. . .

SHOT: CLOSE-UP: on Cousin w/Purple Headband.

COUSIN (PH): *(Looking down at Reader with title showing)*
"Good Book?"

. . . .   CUT!

PROPS:

FAK, Backpacks,

Book for Disguised Cousin. *(Actual or homemade cover added)*

Cousins with backpacks. In Line.

Disguise. (Beach hat, sunglasses, Umbrella, beach chair, cold drink, Book, etc.)

CAMERA PERSON: Please consider downloading each scene after filming, or at end of day to a computer to avoid accidental deleting of completed scenes.

ADD MORE SCENES AS NEEDED. OR AS YOU HAVE COUSINS! OR DO DUO COUSINS.

DIRECTOR'S NOTES:

Check out a copy of "War & Peace" from library, or locate at a used book store or make a fake cover for a thick book.

TIME ESTIMATE:
- --Make-up   0
- --Set-up   5
- --Run throughs   5
- --Video shoots   5
- TOTAL   15 min.

Scene 5b: Fisherman at the Dock

SLUGLINE: EXT., on dock.

DIALOGUE WALK-THROUGH:

SHOT: Wide view of area: cousins approach down the ramp in line.

((First Cousin (different than before) carries First Aid kit, DC at rear of line . . . Off-camera . . . drops out . . . completes disguise.))

| COUSINS: | "Do you see anything?" | : "No. Do you?" |
| | : "No, nothing." | : "Hmmm." |

DC/Fisherman: (*Hard of hearing. Seated, w/fishing pole and line in Water.*)

COUSINS: (*Round the corner, surprised.*) : "Oh! Hello."

DC: (*Does not react. Hard of hearing.*)

| COUSINS: (*Whisper.*) | : "I guess he can't hear." | : "We have to ask." |
| | : "You talk to him." | : "Sir . . . Sir! . . . Sir!!" |

DC: "Huh?"

COUSIN: (*Speaking loudly.*) "Sir! Have you seen our parents? We've lost them!"

DC: (*Cupping hand at his ear.*) "Carrots? You've lost your carrots?"

COUSIN ALL: "No! Our Parents! We can't find them. Have you seen them?

DC *Frowns, puts up open hand* : What do they look like?

COUSINS: : "My dad! . . . always has chapstick in his pocket!

: "My mom! . . . always carries a great big purse!

: "My dad! . . . really likes to go fishing!"

: "My mom! . . . hates a big purse, hers is this big!" (motions w/hands)

DC: (shakes his head, thinking): "Nope. Haven't seen 'em."

"You might look at the beach?"

SHOT: (Close-up) **PHB COUSIN:** "Again?"   CUT!

PROPS:

Fishing Pole/put in place b/f shoot, FAK.

Cousins with backpacks. In Line.

DC disguise: in Backpack.

CAMERA PERSON:

Please consider downloading each scene after filming, or at end of day to a computer to avoid accidental deleting of completed scenes.

DIRECTOR'S NOTES:

TIME ESTIMATE: 15 min.

Scene 6: Birdwatcher   Location:_____   Time:_____

SLUGLINE: EXT.: near trees in background
DIALOGUE: WALK-THRU

SHOT: Wide view of area. (*Cousins approaching, in line. .looking down/clues*)
((*First Cousin (different one than before) carries First Aid kit, another cousin, at rear of line. . .Off camera. DC drops out/completes disguise.*))

COUSINS: (*Looking down.*)   : "Do you see any clues?"

: "No. Do you?"

: "No, nothing."

: "Hmmm."

(*DC: disguised as Birdwatcher; scanning the tree line, Walking without looking. Bumps into line of cousins. Scans them with binoculars before speaking.*)

COUSINS: "Uh-oh! . . . Sorry, sir/ma'am."

"Are you OK, sir/ma'am?"

DC: "Shh. (*Whispers.*) I'm looking for birds. Specifically, the red-breasted, yellow-beaked woodpecker with a purple eye-streak. Have you seen him?

COUSINS: (*ALL Whispering*): "No, sir/ma'am."

(*Stage whispers.*)

: "We're looking for our parents."

: "Maybe you have seen them?"

: "They've been kidnapped."

: "We've looked everywhere!"

DC: (*in character & voice*): "What do they look like?"

COUSINS: : "My dad is . . . this tall!"

: "My mom . . . is this tall!"

: "My dad is this tall and this big around!"

: "My mother . . . is about, hmmm, this tall!"

DC: (*in character/voice*): "Nope. Haven't seen them. . . "Why don't you look at the boat dock?"

SHOT: Close-up on Cousin w/PHB.

PHB: Is this what you call a Wild Goose chase?

DIRECTOR'S NOTES:

TIME ESTIMATE:
15 min.

PROPS:

Binoculars, FAK,

Cousins with backpacks. In Line.

Disguise: binoculars (Carry in Backpack, only for scene when needed, they're heavy.)

CAMERA PERSON:

Please consider downloading each scene after filming, or at end of day to a computer to avoid accidental deleting of completed scenes.

Scene 7: Music Video at the Beach *(Intermission)*

Location: _____ Time: _____

SLUGLINE: EXT., at the Beach,

SHOT: (Make a music video.)

WIDE ANGLE: In the water, singing "Dynamite."

Human Pyramid: singing "Dynamite."

On the beach: dancing, playing Leap Frog, etc,

SHOT: CLOSE UP: dialogue

COUSINS: *(Making sandwiches, filling plates, etc.)*

 : "Shouldn't we go find our parents?"

 : "We will."

 : "Let's eat first.

 : "I'm starving."

 : "What's for drinks?"

(Rocking. At picnic table eating lunch, singing "Dynamite.")

(Singing continues to "cut".)

CAMERA SHOT: (Close up)

COUSIN w/PURPLE HEADBAND: (*Winks.*) "We'll find them."

     . . . . . CUT!

PROPS:

Tape Player or Cell phone app with "Dynamite!" OR other SONG OF YOUR CHOICE.

First Aid Kit

Purple Head Band

CAMERA PERSON:

Please consider downloading each scene after filming, or at end of day to a computer to avoid accidental deleting of completed scenes.

DIRECTOR'S NOTES:

Practice the song. FREE PLAY AT THE BEACH AFTER PICNIC LUNCH.

PHB: Has a line.

TIME ESTIMATE:

--Make-up	0
--Set-up	0
--Transitions x 3	15
--Video shoots x 3	15
TOTAL	30 min.

Scene 8a: Encounter with The Pillow People

SLUGLINE: EXT, woods: Location:_____   Time:_____

WALK-THROUGH, DIALOGUE, BLOCKING:

SHOT: Wide view: Side view of all cousins marching R-L Woods in background.

COUSINS: *(Approaching through the woods slowly; #1 Cousin (not Youngest) struggles to carry the First Aid kit, as if too heavy.)*

SHOT: *(Closer focus. Medium distance.)*

COUSIN 1: *(1ST Cousin stops, drops 1st Aid Kit, POINTS in distance.)*
—: "Look!"
: "Where?"
: "Up ahead."
: "Who are they?"
: "WHAT are they?"

SHOT: *(Close Up on FIRST Cousin.)*

COUSIN 1: "They're the monsters who kidnapped our parents!" . . .

SHOT: *(Widens to All Cousins.)*

ALL: *(Immediately enraged, aggressive, loud, BUT IN PLACE. Yelling at the monsters ahead. Shaking fists . . .)*
: "Where are our parents?"
: "Give us back our parents!"
: "What have you done to our parents?"
: "You mean old monsters!"
: "Let's beat the stuffing out of them!"

SHOT: *(Still side view.)*

(COUSINS begin running toward "Pillow People.")

SHOT: *(Pans left ahead of Cousins.)*

                                                        CUT!

(Allow space on film to splice Sc. 8c here.)

PROPS:

Pillowcases, one each; painted at Craft Time/Day 1.
With eye cut outs.
Faces drawn on, large scale.
(IN BACKPACK!)

First Aid Kit & Purple headband Cousins with backpacks in line. Wearing Belts w/Water Bottles.

EDITING REQUIRED:

Film 8b Next: because in same costume. Final edit: splice 8c with cousins in "Pillow People" costumes to be between 8a & 8b.

DIRECTOR'S NOTES:

REMEMBER:
((Every Scene: Different Cousin carries FAK.))

((Every Scene: Different Cousin wears Purple Head Band.))

TIME ESTIMATE:
--Run throughs   10
--Video shoots   5
TOTAL   15 min.

Scene 8b: "They're Not the Enemy" *(Edit Req'd)*

SLUGLINE: EXT., same as Scene 8a ends:

SHOT: Wide view. Pans right w/cousins marching left to right, sleepily.

(Cousins REVERSE, now marching back where they came from, L-R. now.)
(Cousin w/FAK falling behind, still struggles with big Suitcase.)

(Singing & yawning: "Cousin Camp" song: "Cousins...at...Camp... Who... sing...off-key...)

SHOT: Close-up of Cousin w/PHB.
    LAST COUSIN: *(Covers his/her mouth to yawn.)* "I guess they're not the enemy."

SHOT: Panning out to all cousins, Side view.
    ... We're...poor...little...frogs...who...have...lost... Our... parents...Rivet...Rivet...Rivet! . . . .
                       . . . .   CUT!

(Continue to Scene 8c)

PROPS:
Cousins in Line with Backpacks. With First Aid Kit.

DIRECTOR'S NOTES:

Scene 8c: Encounter with the Pillow People

SLUGLINE: EXT., woods: Location:_____ Time:_____

DIALOGUE RUN-THROUGH! (b/f costume change)

COSTUME CHANGE! (Assemble in a circle in open area.)

(PILLOW PEOPLE, playing Ring-Around-the-Rosey (SLOWLY) moving in a circle.)

(SOUND CHECK!)

SHOT: Wide view, whole circle of Pillow People

COUSINS: *(Disguise their voices. Sing-song. Slow-ly)* "Ring— ar-ound—the—Ros-ey, . . . Pock-et—full—of—pos-ies!— (x2)

COUSINS: (Talk slowly like they're sleepy.)
: "Hey! Who's..that..coming..toward..us?
: "They..don't..look..very.. friendly."
: "They..look..mean!"
: "I..think..they're..attack.ing..us!"
: "Quick!..Let's..sing..a..lull-a-by."

(One cousin leads, singing each line/making up the tune or to tune of "Rock-a-by-Baby." Leader pauses. Others repeat in same tune.)

SHOT: Closer in.

COUSIN Leader: (Singing slowly and softly, swaying in a relaxing, hypnotic action.)

CHORUS: ✱ : "We're..really..not..the..enemy // ...   .
: "We're..soft..and..cuddly..don't..you..see?   (Al fine.)
: "At..night..we..put..you..to-o..sleep.   ...   ...
: "We..really..are..a..friend..to-o..keep.   ...   ...
: "A faithful fri-end for your sleep . . .   . . .
: "Your dreams are where we help count sheep.   ...   ...

REPEAT CHORUS   . . . .   CUT!

DIALOGUE RUN-THRU

COSTUME CHANGE
    Pillow People Costumes IN BACKPACK.

SOUND CHECK:
Test the sound before recording the whole scene. May require all shots to be close-ups for camera to PU sound adequately. MAKE ADJUSTMENTS.

Editor: This scene Sc8.c will be SPLICED to end of Sc8.a. Sc8.b will be SPLICED onto this scene, Sc.8.c.
This will complete the episode with Pillow People.

8a: Cousins see Pillow People Ahead

8c: Pillow People see Cousins coming to fight. Singing a lullaby is their defense.

8b: Cousins return. "Pillow People" are not the enemy.

DIRECTOR'S NOTES:

TIME ESTIMATE:
--Make-up   0
--Set-up   0
--Transitions x 3   15
--Video shoots x 3   15
TOTAL   30 min.